MW00490584

15 Months of Winter
My Year in North Dakota

John Bayer

To Michael,
Happy Reading!
John Bayer

 Melicrate Press

To the Divide County Public Library,
the Burbank Public Library
and the libraries throughout the nation
that provide their communities with the
most valuable resources on earth:
information, language, and ideas.

CONTENTS

ACKNOWLEDGMENTS

My sincere thanks go out to the following people:

To Holly R. Anderson for saying "move to Crosby," when I told her I needed to get away from Los Angeles.

To Arlene Anderson for giving up her home so that I had a place to live. Please don't sue me.

To Cecile Krimm for hiring some stranger from California to work for her newspaper and for taking a chance on the *O! Pioneer* column in the first place.

To Steve Andrist not for anything specific, but I'm hoping that he'll buy a book if he knows his name is in it.

To Guyla Mills for serving as my editor—helping me to organize my thoughts and to see things in new ways. You were a constant source of encouragement.

To Kyle Jones for creating the cover, and making this thing look like a real book.

To my readers, Sidney Showers and John Taylor for catching my abundant spelling and grammatical errors. Yu died a grate job!

To Mitch Lusas for assistance with the book layout.

To everyone who contributed their great photographs to the book.

To my parents, John and Lois Bayer, for investing in this little business venture, called *John Bayer, Writer, Inc.*

To my sister Jonell Bayer, for having the good taste to think everything I say or write is funny.

To the people of North Dakota, and specifically the city of Crosby, for welcoming me in and giving me a place to call "my home away from civilization."

To all of those who wrote letters, sent emails or stopped me on the street to say, "I enjoy reading *O! Pioneer.*" It was you who gave me the courage to step out and write this. If you don't like the book, you have only yourselves to blame.

INTRODUCTION/CONFESSIONS

I have a few confessions to make.

The first one is this: I lived in North Dakota for 428 days. That's more than a year, which is the time period stated in the book's subtitle. But it's also less than the 15 months that my main title states. Basically, I'm a liar all around.

For the official record, I lived in North Dakota from July 2012 to September 2013.

I moved to Crosby, North Dakota because I needed adventure and new experiences. And by "adventure" I mean "money." And by "new experiences" I mean "to get the flip out of Los Angeles." What brought me to Los Angeles in the first place was the desire to be a writer. In four short years, the City of Angels had left me in debt, in depression and in creative paralysis.

A former classmate of mine from film school, Holly (*we're just friends*), recommended I move to the Peace Garden State. I had a better idea—I would move to her home state of North Dakota. I was later informed that North Dakota *is* the Peace Garden State.

I came with a strategy: live in North Dakota for a year, write a book about my experiences, and make lots of money. Two out of three ain't bad. Or as some North Dakotans say, "It's better than a poke in the eye with a sharp stick."

My second confession: Winter is the most beautiful season of the year in North Dakota. I'll repeat that. Winter is the most beautiful season in North Dakota. By far.

Again, that might not seem like too much of a confession, but for those familiar with my *O! Pioneer* columns, you know that's not the kind of thing I would say. At this point you're wondering if this is the setup for a joke, or if I'm having someone else write this book for me, or if I'm just drunk.

The answer of course is: it's all three.

It happens to be true though. Winter in North Dakota is beautiful. You might have to hunker down in your house for an entire day while a blizzard hits. But the next day you step outside and the world is white and shiny and pristine. It's a wondrous sight.

Locals downplay blizzards by calling them "winter storms." Conversely, I lovingly refer to the two heaviest winter storms of that year as "Snowmaggedon" and "the Snowpocalypse."

Then there are the trees. In the winter, moisture in the air comes in contact with the trees and turns into frost. The tree basically becomes encased in ice—making it white and shimmery. That's a paltry description of something that took my breath away the first time I saw it. The tree outside my place, that I'd walked past for months, had been transformed into a completely new thing—something out of a fairy tale, out of a child's imagination. I'd never seen anything like it.

I could give more examples, but you get the idea. Winter in North Dakota is lovely and nice and good. But as the saying goes, all good things must come to an end.

Except when they don't end. Like winter in North Dakota.

This book is called *15 Months of Winter*. That's a jokey title and not at all true. The truth is, winter in North Dakota never ends. There may only be snow on the ground for seven months of the year ("only!"), but the North Dakota winter never leaves you. It goes with you long after you've left the state. Weather-induced post-traumatic stress disorder. It clings to your heart and your mind like a parasite that wants to take everything good or beautiful, and freeze it out until all you can do is just scream, and then you get strange looks from the other people standing in the checkout line with you at Target. You scream but it's no comfort. The pain is still there. And will always be. . .

North Dakota in autumn is nice too.

My third confession: Everything wrong in my life is North Dakota's fault. I save the biggest confessions for last.

Basically, my life is a complete and total wreck. Now a weaker person might blame himself for this state of affairs, but experts agree that in our most difficult times it's important to look outside ourselves. So I look at my mess of a life and see North Dakota's fingerprints all over it.

I was originally going to call this book *Blame North Dakota*, but I worried that title might not sell well in the Midwest.

Let me give you a few examples: I don't have a girlfriend. I can't drive on freeways. I'm 40 pounds overweight, give or take 50 pounds. These things are all obviously North Dakota's fault.

Now some people who know me well might point out that I didn't have a girlfriend, and I couldn't drive on freeways, and that I was overweight long before I moved to North Dakota.

I'm not saying North Dakota is the reason I have these problems. I'm saying that North Dakota is the reason I *still* have these problems.

I broke my ankle shortly after moving to North Dakota. It was my first broken bone ever. *Thanks North Dakota!* That caused my activity level to go down quite a bit—which caused me to eat more—which caused me to put on an additional 40 pounds while living up north.

The best way to overcome a fear of freeways is just get out there and drive on freeways as much as possible. But there is only one freeway in North Dakota, and it's in the south of the state—four hours away from where I was.

And there's not much opportunity for romance either. Again, I know I need to get out there. But there is only one single woman in North Dakota and she's right next to the freeway.

There are other things wrong in my life. I won't go into them. I'd like to keep a little bit of mystery between us. Suffice it to say: all of those problems are North Dakota's fault too.

This is not just a blind accusation. I have evidence. Every other place I've lived—but particularly Los Angeles—has been interested in the improvement of the person. You're overweight and have a poor body image? Eat right and exercise, maybe see a counselor. You get panic attacks driving on the interstate? Just get out there, try immersion therapy, maybe see a counselor. You're shy asking women out? Just get out there, try immersion therapy, maybe see a counselor. A lot of counselors are single, lonely women.

In North Dakota, they aren't as concerned with the parts as they are with the whole. You're fat? That's okay, as long as you're still able to get your big backside to work every day. You're afraid of freeways? Well, I suppose the community will still be able to function. You're afraid of women? You're sure afraid of a lot of stuff. Good thing there aren't any women out in that field, we've got a crop to bring in.

I can't sleep tonight. It's you-know-who's fault.

I'm back in Los Angeles. It's my first night sleeping in my new bedroom. Which as it happens is actually my old bedroom. I'm right back in the same apartment that I lived in before I left LA. It's the same, but it's different. For one thing, I don't have any furniture. I sold all my furniture before I moved up to North Dakota. It's just me and my air mattress and my folding chair right now. It looks like I've been robbed. The person who moved into this place after me did a lot of upgrades—installing two ceiling fans, adding built-in shelves, having the landlord put down new carpet and tiles. The bathroom has been completely redone. It's as if my place has been robbed, but the thieves stuck around afterwards to make some home improvements.

I settle into my air mattress. It's comfortable enough, but I can't sleep. Los Angeles is too noisy. I am overwhelmed by the sound of cars as they drive by on the busy street, 40 feet away. They almost sound like they're in the room with me.

Were the cars always this loud? I lived here for two years before and I don't remember them being this loud. Has the apartment moved closer to the street? I get up and check the windows to make sure they're not open. They're closed.

I wonder if I'll ever get used to this noise. Again. I wonder if I'll get any sleep tonight.

My place in North Dakota was always quiet. Except for the birds that would start chirping a good hour before the sun came up. A lot of people love the sounds of birds singing. I'm not one of those people. Many mornings, I would have given money for the traffic of LA—either to drown out the relentless chirping, or to at least run over the birds who weren't on their toes.

But that was in the morning. During the night, all was quiet—except for the 10 p.m. air raid siren in the center of town which rang out every night for no discernible reason. The loud thirty-second daily blare—Crosby's way of saying "IT IS 10 O'CLOCK. YOU MAY NOW ENTER INTO A PEACEFUL WORLD OF SLUMBER. THAT IS ALL."

North Dakota has ruined me. I've grown too accustomed to the silence to sleep here anymore. And also, lying here in the dark, there's no way of knowing if it's 10 o'clock yet.

During my year in North Dakota, there were two weeks in the middle of winter where the temperature got so low even the siren was too cold to sound. The siren simply froze up. God bless North Dakota winters! (What am I saying? I don't know who I am anymore.)

The siren—piercing the sky every day at noon and again at ten at night —reminds me a lot of the North Dakotans I've come to know over the last year. They aren't particularly loud, unlike the siren, but they're determined and persistent. They're also consistent. You can set your watch by most North Dakotans. Go ahead, they won't mind. At times, they behave in ways that make sense to no one but themselves. If that.

And though North Dakotans would never admit it to an outsider, even they take a few weeks here and there to slow down or even stop what they're doing when the worst of the winter hits—just like that siren.

This book is a collection of essays written about my time in Crosby, North Dakota, a near-idyllic city of about 1100 people in the northwest corner of the state, and on the edge of the current oil boom. Many of these essays originally appeared in *O! Pioneer*, a humor column I wrote during my time in North Dakota. These columns ran about twice a month in two weekly newspapers—*The Journal* (of Divide County) and *The Tioga Tribune*.

The rest of the essays are from my notes during that time. These never made it into the column for various reasons: too long, too short, no space in the paper to run them. Or maybe they just weren't funny. I guess you'll find out.

Thank you for picking up this book. Come with me now as I take you on an amazing journey of self-discovery. During the course of this book, you'll begin to question everything you ever knew about love, life, and the very nature of the fabric that holds it all together; then you'll receive answers to all of those questions; then you'll forget those answers completely. After this, you'll start to get hungry, so you'll set the book down to get a snack. When you return to the book, you'll begin to remember all of the answers to the questions of life; but they will be in Norwegian. But you don't speak or understand Norwegian! Except now suddenly you do!

So, in a nutshell, this is my promise to you: By the time you finish reading this book, you will have answers to the most profound existential questions that have plagued mankind throughout time and you will speak

Norwegian.

Failing that, I hope you'll gain a little insight into the lives of the people of the great state of North Dakota, and see that they're just regular people. Except when they're not. And I hope you'll laugh a little along the way.

At the very least, I hope reading this book is better than a poke in the eye with a sharp stick.

And if it isn't, it's North Dakota's fault.

photo: Gary M. Joraanstad

Downtown Crosby, North Dakota

NORTH DAKOTA DICTIONARY

Here is a list of words or phrases one should learn in order to survive in North Dakota.

Some of these terms are local colloquialisms.

Others are Norwegian words. Many of the people who settled North Dakota during the homestead period were of Norwegian lineage. Today's North Dakotans still identify themselves as Norwegians. I suspect this is because it's so cold there, these people don't realize they are no longer in Norway.

The entries in this dictionary aren't in alphabetical order because they try not to put on airs in the Midwest, but are rather in which-words-I-thought-up-first-ical order.

Learning these terms will help you get along more easily in North Dakota, and should make this book a little easier to understand. That's not guaranteed, though.

AG – pronounced "egg". Short for Agriculture. North Dakotans do not like long words – unless they are impossible to pronounce Norwegian words —and they will abbreviate (shorten) these words whenever possible. (See "C-Store") I never learned if North Dakotans have an abbreviation for North Dakotan.

THE CITIES – Another example of shortening: In Minnesota, there are two well-known cities called St. Paul and Minneapolis. But Americans are too lazy to say "St. Paul and Minneapolis" all of the time, so they say "The Twin Cities." Not to be outdone by the rest of the country, the people in the North Dakota neck of the woods one-up the lazy by referring to "The Cities." This may just happen in western North Dakota, but I suspect it's a Midwest thing. When I'm having a particularly rough day and don't feel like talking I just refer to Minneapolis-St. Paul as "The."

BARS – Women in North Dakota are obsessed with bars. Not the buildings with liquor in them. I'm referring to the kind you make. There's nothing in the world that gives a North Dakota woman more pleasure than pressing oats covered in peanut butter into a 9"x13" baking dish, drizzling chocolate over it, baking it at 350 degrees for 25 minutes and then cutting the resulting confection into smaller rectangles.

In years when the Olympics are held, you will see a lot of "official" commercials. Spring Mountain is the Official Water of the U.S. Women's Gymnastics Team. Steinberg is the Official Grand Piano of the U.S. Track and Field Team. DriNow is the Official Feminine Hygiene product of the U.S. Men's Basketball Team. You get the idea.

Bars are the Official Handheld Rectangular Dessert of the Midwest. They are served at every fundraising, social, and community event.

During my time in North Dakota, I served on a committee hell-bent on trying to bring the arts to the area. For one of our events, we decided we wanted to do something a little classier than our usual fare; so we threw a Champagne Gala. We didn't have a huge turnout—but boy, those bars shaped like champagne flutes were delicious!

Meanwhile, the men in North Dakota are obsessed with those buildings with liquor in them.

SAKAKAWEA – pronounced "Suh-KAK-uh-way-uh." This is the real name of the woman who served as a guide for Lewis and Clark. The rest of the world calls this Native American history maker "Sacajawea." The rest of the world is wrong! Ask any North Dakotan. If you're caught in North Dakota carrying a Sacajawea dollar coin, you're publicly flogged.

BOXELDER BUGS – These are black and red bugs—about a half inch long —that primarily show themselves during the autumn in North Dakota. Boxelder bugs got the name because they supposedly live in boxelder trees. I've never seen a boxelder bug in a tree. You know how some people have outside dogs and some people have inside dogs? Well, the boxelder is most definitely an inside bug. They prefer a split level, three bedroom bungalow near the center of town, but they'll take whatever they can get. They are a little strapped for cash right now, so they're going to move in with you for a little while. All three million of them.

Boxelder bugs are harmless, but they can definitely stain your home if you squash too many of them in the same spot. Boxelder bugs have wings but they generally reserve flying for special occasions. Shortly after the first snowfall of the year, all of the boxelder bugs suddenly move out of your house. Presumably, they have taken the first bus to Albuquerque. It is the one and only good thing about a North Dakota winter.

C-STORE – This is how North Dakotans say "Convenience Store." For the longest time, I thought people were saying "seed store" as in: "John, I'm going down to the seed store. Do you need me to get you anything?" "Um, no. I'm good. All my seed needs are well in hand. Thank you."

DINNER – Lunch

SUPPER – Dinner

LUNCH – Any time you're just snacking. If you're eating a bar, it's lunch.

NORSK HOSTFEST – The nation's largest Scandinavian heritage festival in the United States, held every October in Minot, North Dakota. Unfortunately, I never got the opportunity to attend so I can't really comment on it. Except to say, it's a really big deal.

Among the entertainers at the 2013 Norsk Hostfest celebrating Scandinavian culture were: Frank Sinatra, Jr., the country band Alabama, and Bill Cosby (who I believe is Finnish).

POP – Every region has its favorite word for carbonated sugar water—soda, cola, coke and in North Dakota, it's "pop." Eighty percent of the people here drink diet pop, which I never found a rhyme or reason for other than some things just are.

HOT DISH – In the Eastern United States, people throw away expired food. In the West, it's all microbiotic nonsense, so it's impossible to tell when food's gone bad. In the Midwest, they put expired food in a baking dish, add a can of green beans, a can of cream of mushroom soup and a prayer to the Almighty and call it hot dish.

When an outsider asks a North Dakotan, "What is hot dish?" for the sake of simplicity the Dakotan will answer, "It's another name for a casserole." Whenever this happens, every casserole on the planet dies a little more inside.

Hot dish is not a casserole. Hot dish is like a casserole, only it's wetter and paler. And it doesn't quite taste like any of the things that were put into it. Hot dish is casserole's dim-witted toothless cousin that casserole hides up in the attic whenever company comes over.

LEFSE – pronouced "LEF-sah." A Scandinavian dessert. It is a flat disc made from a combination of potato flour and wheat flour. I once made the mistake of saying that lefse looks vaguely like a tortilla – an grievous error for which I was publicly shunned. Lefse is best right off the grill, slathered with butter and sugar (maybe cinnamon), then folded up and consumed right then and there. Fresh lefse covered in butter and sugar tastes like warm butter and sugar. At its best lefse doesn't really taste like much of anything—it mostly serves as the conduit through which sugar and butter are transmitted to the body.

Lukewarm or cold lefse, on the other hand, tastes like sadness. It has an unpleasant starchiness to it. Like eating a can of soggy Pringles.

LUTEFISK – pronounced "LOU-tah-fisk." A stinky, gelatinous mound that was once fish. Lutefisk is a Norwegian delicacy. And by delicacy, I mean there isn't enough money on the planet to pay someone to eat it all of the time. As a general rule, everyone hates lutefisk but they'll eat it once a year for the sake of tradition. There is a small minority of people who actually like lutefisk, but even they hate lutefisk.

Generally, lutefisk takes between 10 and 14 days to prepare. This ordeal begins with a salted, dried cod which is soaked in cold water for four to six days. After this, the cod spends two days in a cold lye bath, followed by another four to six days in cold water. The resulting mass is then covered in salt to remove moisture, then rinsed to remove salt, then steamed or boiled to remove any remaining taste. The fact that this process is ever undertaken, and that the finished product is ever consumed is proof that Norwegians have a great sense of humor.

Lutefisk is generally eaten once a year, around Christmastime. What better way to celebrate our Savior's birth than with stomach cramps? I feel it would be more appropriate to serve lutefisk on Good Friday—so that we could share in Christ's sufferings. Most Norwegians are Lutherans. Whereas Catholics have penance, Lutherans have lutefisk.

LUDEFEST – This is an annual festival that Concordia Lutheran Church in Crosby used to put on in the fall to celebrate the wonder that is lutefisk. My year in North Dakota was the first year they had to cancel the festival because there was no one to organize the event. Cancelling Ludefest was a great disappointment for the community, and a bit of a relief for the individuals that make up the community.

SPICE RACK – That place where you keep the salt and pepper shakers.

SONS OF NORWAY – This is a fraternal organization of some sort. The only thing I really know about the Sons of Norway is that 80 percent of the members are women.

UFF DA – pronounced "OOF-dah." This is by far my favorite North Dakota word. I use it all the time. It's also the word I get asked about the most. Uff da (spelled "oof dah" by the ignorant and by people who live in Montana) is used quite commonly in the upper Midwest, but no one outside of the region seems to have ever heard it. Let me educate you.

Uff da is a Norwegian-American term that means, well, "uff da." It's hard to explain exactly what it means. If it's winter and you slip on the ice but somehow manage not to fall, you would say "UFF DA," meaning "that was a close one." If you slip on the ice and still fall on your butt, you would say a more subdued "uff da" to mean "well, I went and done it now." If the Zombie Apocalypse came and you were surrounded on all sides by the living dead who desired to eat your brains and you had absolutely no means of escape, you would say "UFF da" which is loosely translated into "we've really stepped into some horse-shucks here."

Uff da is the word that you say when you just can't say anything else. It's almost the Scandinavian equivalent to the Yiddish phrase "Oy vey."

There's an episode of the 80s sitcom *The Golden Girls*, where Rose is visited by three men from her hometown of St. Olaf, Minnesota to congratulate her on being the town's Woman of the Year. At one point the men raise their glasses to her in a toast, and proclaim "Uff da." Whoever wrote this episode didn't do his homework.

Uff da is never a celebratory term. The closest it comes is when you are extremely overweight and you say "uff da" after you've managed to successfully lift yourself out of your chair. That's it. Norwegians are not by nature a celebratory people. Celebration draws too much attention. Norwegians like to remain unseen, hidden, stealthy. That's why so many famous ninjas have been Norwegian.

LAY OF THE LAND

Most Americans would not be able to identify North Dakota on a map—even on a map where the states are clearly labeled. In California and New York, they aren't aware that all those spaces in the middle even have individual names. Thankfully, I am here to educate the ignorant. Let's begin.

Here is a map of the United States drawn to precise scale:

Up there at the top ("America's freezer") and about halfway left to right is North Dakota.

Here's how the state looks close up.

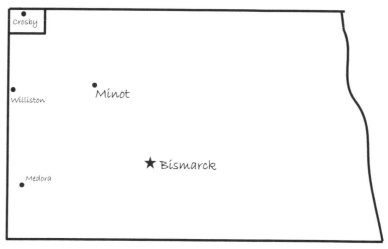

North Dakota

The state capital is Bismarck. If you're new around here, then the first time you spell that state capital, you'll write Bismark—forgetting the "c." It's a mistake everyone makes. But only once, if they know what's good for them.

A hundred miles north and west of Bismarck is the city of Minot. According to the website, www.minotnd.org, the town has a population of 40,888 people. Also, according to the website, the city is at an elevation of 1,631 feet and is located at the following coordinates: Latitude, 48 degrees, 18 minutes North; Longitude, 101 degrees, 20 minutes West.

Minot is the home to the North Dakota State Fair, the Norsk Hostfest Scandinavian Festival, the nation's most cumbersome international airport, and actor Josh Duhamel.

Close to the Montana border is Williston. That city's website won't tell me the population, or the elevation, or even the longitude! So I don't have much to say about Williston. Williston is a good sized city—meaning it has a Wal-Mart. It's only an hour from the small town where I lived. When people in Crosby needed to get away, though, they'd make the two hour drive to Minot over the shorter Williston drive. Williston is in the heart of the oil boom and the city has become congested and dirty.

I once received an email from someone who had transposed the 's' and the second 'i' in Williston, so that it read "Will sit on." That has nothing to do with anything, but I thought it was funny. Still do.

Further down, in the southwest corner of the state is the town of Medora. Although you've never heard of it, Medora is the largest tourist attraction in North Dakota. The town was founded in the 1800s by a Frenchman named Antoine-Amédée-Marie-Vincent Manca Amat de Vallombrosa, Marquis de Morés et de Montemaggiore who fancied himself a cattlemen. (Seriously, that was his name.) When he came to settle in North Dakota, he thankfully named the town after his wife instead of after himself.

Medora is a tourist town. It's one part Old West town, two parts country western revue, and one part Teddy Roosevelt tribute museum. With just a dash of Disneyland tossed in for good measure.

Now let's move north, to the upper corner of the state, where you'll find Crosby, North Dakota in Divide County. This was my home away from civilization. Here's a closer view of Divide County:

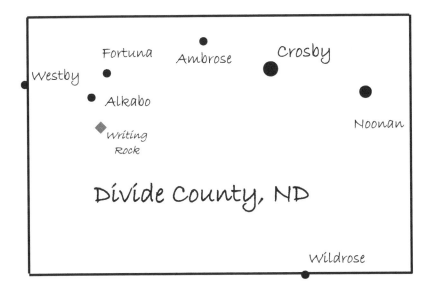

Divide County is in the northwesternmost corner of the state, with the mysterious land of Canada above it and the even more mysterious land of Montana to the west of it. Divide County is composed of five towns: Crosby, Noonan, Ambrose, Alkabo and Fortuna.

Crosby is the largest city with 1,100 residents. It serves as the county seat and has its own country club with a 9-hole golf course open whenever it's warm enough to golf—about two and half weeks out of the year.

The next largest town is Noonan at around 300 (give or take 50). Noonan has a pretty active chapter of the Lion's Club—Crosby is strictly Moose country—and also lays claim to the best (by virtue of being the only) Mexican restaurant in Divide County.

The other towns in Divide County are teeny tiny, but I would guess that Alkabo has the most people of the three. I'm pretty sure that Fortuna is just some guy with a couple of hunting dogs that he claims as dependents on his tax return.

South of Alkabo is a state historical site called Writing Rock. It's basically two big stones tagged with ancient graffiti. No one knows who carved the images onto the rocks—presumably Native Americans, but the tribe is a mystery—and no one knows what the images mean. They keep the stones in a little cage next to a guest book for visitors to sign. Here's my sister at Writing Rock:

photo: John Bayer

You may have noticed from the Divide County map two other towns: Wildrose and Westby. I list them because every map of Divide County that I've ever seen have included Wildrose and Westby. I don't know why that's the case because these towns aren't in Divide County. Wildrose is in Williams County. I've been told a little bit of the town spills over into Divide County, so technically it might belong on the Divide map. That "little bit" must consist of someone's tool shed, because Wildrose is small.

And Westby. Not only is Westby not in Divide County; it isn't even in the state of North Dakota! It's in Montana. I read or heard somewhere that Westby was once in North Dakota. At one point North Dakota passed a prohibition law, but the people in Westby wanted to keep drinking; so they moved the town into Montana. This seems kind of far-fetched but then again, why would a town in *east*ern Montana be called *West*by?

If Westby used to be in North Dakota, that also explains why it's on their maps. If I've learned anything about North Dakota, it's this: once something is named something or written a certain way, it will be forever named that thing or written that way. There used to be a J.C. Penney store in Crosby. It closed in the mid-1980s. Many different businesses have been located in that building over the past three decades. Locals still call it "the Penney Building"—so if you're a stranger in town and need directions, don't ask a local.

In order to understand North Dakota, I think it's important to go back. Across the Atlantic Ocean to where it all began:

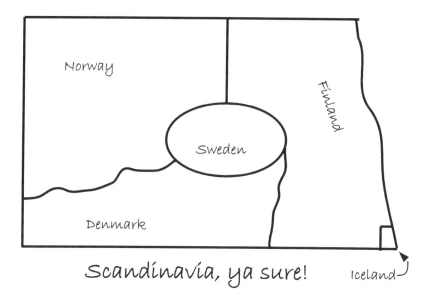

Scandinavia, ya sure!

This is Scandinavia, a region in Europe or Asia or someplace like that. A significant percentage of North Dakota's population is people of Scandinavian heritage.

Do you notice how similar Scandinavia looks to North Dakota? I think that's the main reason why so many Scandinavian people settled here during the Homestead period, which happened sometime before I was born.

Scandinavia is comprised of five countries: Norway, Sweden, Denmark, Finland and Iceland. Iceland is on the fringe. It's sort of like the letter Y. Sometimes it's a Scandinavian country and sometimes you forget it's a real place at all and not some fairy land that J.R.R. Tolkien created.

Though joined by common ancestry, each of these five countries has its own distinctly rich culture, history and people—none of which we will concern ourselves with.

Norway is the area of our primary interest. A large portion of Divide County's population is made up of Norwegians. If you're considering becoming a humorist, I highly recommend living among Norwegians. You will never run out of material.

Although I like to pick on the Norwegians, I want to point out that they weren't the only nationality represented during the homestead period. Quite a few homesteading families originated from Germany:

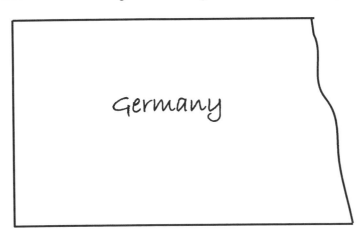

I won't be spending much time making fun of Germans. They don't take jokes at their own expense so well. (e.g.: World War I, World War II)

Homesteaders also came to North Dakota from wherever Belgian people come from.

Are the people Belgian and the country Belgium? Or are the people Belgium and the country Belgian? Who knows, but I could really go for a waffle.

photo: Jonell Bayer

STRAWBERRY FIELDS FOREVER
from notes dated 7/18/2012

I'm one of the lucky ones. I have an affordable place to stay. Most of the new people coming to North Dakota aren't as fortunate. There's been such a massive influx of new people into the western half of the state over the last few years, and there simply isn't an infrastructure in place to handle it.

This is a place that's accustomed to folks going out rather than coming in. On the great seal of North Dakota are inscribed the words, "Sorry to see you leave already."

But oil has changed all of that. There are people everywhere and no place to stick them. From that first moment I arrived in Crosby, the evidence was there—an RV shanty town on the southern edge of the city. I'm told there's a larger one on the northeast edge of town. The cramped quarters aren't too bad here in July, but it's going to be a hard slog for these folks once winter hits.

There is construction in Crosby—new apartments being built. The people moving into these places will be paying through the nose. Rents here are comparable to those in Los Angeles.

But I'm lucky. Yesterday, I moved into a fully furnished two-bedroom condo for about half the rent of my one-bedroom in LA. It's the home of Holly's mother. Because of health issues, she's had to move in with Holly for a time, which opened up a place for me to live. Very lucky.

"She likes strawberries," Holly told me over the phone a few months ago.

"They are always good on cereal," I agreed.

"You've been warned," she said with a laugh. The laugh grew to a maniacal cackle.

"Okay, see you soon," I replied, oblivious.

I didn't think much more of it until my arrival in North Dakota yesterday. As Holly chauffeured me to my new home in her mother's red car—license plate "STRWBRRY"—I couldn't help but notice three large strawberries painted on the garage.

After saying goodbyes, I plopped down on the couch. It had been a long day of travel and it felt good to finally be where I am going.

I am truly lucky.

I sat on the couch for a while, leaning against the strawberry-themed throw draped across the back and resting my arm on the strawberry embroidered pillow before finally deciding to have a look around. There was so much to take in: the spoon collection, the vast DVD library of Gaither Homecoming videos, the sewing room, and the strawberries. So many strawberries. The strawberry curtains in the living room. The strawberry knick knacks. The strawberry sock puppets.

It hit me. Everything about this place just screams: A single man in his 30s lives here. Lucky me.

I went back to the bathroom to get something for this sudden headache. I opened the cabinet and saw a bottle of Bufferin. "Do they still make Bufferin?" I contemplated donating the ancient bottle with its yellow, faded label to the Smithsonian.

It was then I realized I had learned my first lesson: True North Dakotans never throw anything out. Ever.

I reached for the bottle out of pure fascination. While my fingers were still a half inch away, the label fell off. The glue affixing it had given up the ghost decades ago; the label was just looking for some outside affirmation before deciding to completely disintegrate. I panicked realizing I had destroyed an artifact—my vision of taking the Bufferin to the Antiques Roadshow was dashed. I quickly tossed the bottle into the trash. A slight jangle tells me that there are still pills inside. I quickly threw a few sheets of toilet paper into the trash can to cover my tracks.

I washed my hands, using the regular bar and not the decorative strawberry-shaped soap. Then I made my way to the kitchen. When I flipped the light on, I took a moment to admire the strawberry switch plate. I surveyed the kitchen: strawberry wallpaper, strawberry dish towels, strawberry oven mitts, strawberry soap dispenser, a strawberry ceramic vase holding red ladles and spatulas, a kitchen timer shaped like a strawberry that you set by twisting like a pepper grinder.

I opened the first cabinet to discover plates with a strawberry pattern. "Hmm, I didn't see that coming."

As a child, John Lennon spent many days playing in the gardens of a Salvation Army children's home called "Strawberry Field." Memories of those happy days became the inspiration for the Beatles hit *Strawberry Fields Forever*. Now, in my own little field of strawberries, I pondered what great works of art—song and painting, sculpture and literature—I would be inspired to create here.

I didn't think about that long. I was hungry and I opened more kitchen cabinets in search of food. Thankfully, I found the house well stocked.

I noticed that a date of purchase had been written in black marker on each item.

There are at least 30 boxes of Jell-O on one shelf. The most recent one is marked 07-08, but most of them were purchased in the 90s. The Jell-Oseum goes back as far as 03-87. I took some time to observe how the Jell-O packaging has changed over the last few decades. I decided that I just wasn't in the mood for dessert.

I wasn't sure what I wanted, but narrowed it down to something post-Civil War. A bag of tortilla chips from the early 2000s grabbed my attention. The bag had been opened before, but it had subsequently been resealed with a large clip. So, I figured they were still good.

I took the chips into the living room to watch some TV. I pressed down on the plastic strawberry to open the clip to discover that the bag of chips smelled like chemicals. Chemicals that have been placed in a barn.

I decided to try one of the chips, anyway. The crunch was good, but it had an acrid aftertaste. I should toss these, I thought, but heard a faint voice from the bathroom, "you're in North Dakota now." It was the voice of the Bufferin bottle coming back to haunt me. "We don't just throw things away here," the muffled voice emanating from under the toilet paper chided. I decided to eat the bag, all the while thinking about kids in Africa who don't even have chemical chips to eat.

For the next few hours, I admired a red bath towel with a strawberry in the center, as I sat on the throne and let the chips run their course. I heard snickering from the trash can.

"Oh shut up, you," I commanded.

Later, I pulled back the strawberry comforter from the bed and nestled snugly between the strawberry sheets and the comforter. I rested my head on the strawberry pillow. I looked over to an understated painting of Jesus praying in the Garden of Gethsemene, his two strawberries—where eyes would normally be—gazing up toward heaven.

I gave the Big Guy a quick, "Thank you for bringing me here. I feel very lucky."

Last night, I dreamt that I was in a field and a large combine was approaching. I tried to run, but my feet had turned to roots. I was harvested. The next moment, I was being crushed into jam.

photo: Jonell Bayer

36

THE ADVENTURES OF A CALIFORNIA TRANSPLANT BEGIN

O! Pioneer column originally published 8/15/12

"Why would you want to move to rural North Dakota?"

That was the first question Steve Andrist ever asked me. I was in Los Angeles at the time, talking to Steve and to Cecile Krimm, who were on my computer screen. They were interviewing me long distance for a production job at Journal Publishing. I don't recall my answer to Steve's question. It must have been pretty good, though, because two months later, here I am.

I shouldn't be in North Dakota. It doesn't make any sense. I'm supposed to be a television sitcom writer. My life has been pointing in that direction for some time. I studied writing and theater in college. I went on to film school. I worked for two years as the assistant director of a television program in Virginia. Then a little over four years ago, I made the big move to Los Angeles, the place where all serious comedy writers have to go eventually. I arrived with a full car, an empty wallet, three scripts and the naïve notion that I was going to be an overnight success. I was exactly where I should be. And logically, it's where I should be still.

But after four years, it was no longer where I wanted to be. I was tired. Tired of being unemployed more often than I was employed. I was tired of the noise, the traffic, the congestion. My life in LA had grown old, and it was making me old right along with it.

I needed something new. I needed to rekindle my fire and passion for life; to take on more than I could chew and then get to chewing anyway. What I've come to realize is I needed a little infusion of the Pioneer Spirit.

That Pioneer Spirit (both words must always be capitalized) is in the air and in the soil here. The Pioneer Spirit is what brought explorers here a couple hundred years ago; and the Pioneer Spirit brought the homesteaders after that. Today, the oil boom is drawing many people to the area who are looking for a fresh start for themselves and for their families.

That's why I moved to rural North Dakota. The Pioneer Spirit. I want new adventures. I want to take in and soak up every opportunity this place has to offer me. I want to ride in a thresher. I want to say that I survived a North Dakota winter. I want to explore exotic places like an oil field or a grain elevator. I want to learn the proper usage of the term uffda. (Did I even spell that right?)

Even though writing is not a part of my official job duties at Journal Publishing, I'm hoping that this little column will serve as the first of many where I get the opportunity to share with you my experiences and observations. Because one thing I have in even greater measure than my Pioneer Spirit is my Fragile Ego; which needs you to read my stories and to laugh at my jokes and to like me. Please, please like me.

So to you, the good people of North Dakota, I would like to say: I don't know how long I'll be with you; but I hope that you don't mind being stuck with the pleasure of my company for a while. Because this is exactly where I want to be.

A few early observations

In many ways Southern California and North Dakota are like night and day. But I've noticed in a few subtle ways, they are strikingly similar.

Nobody walks. I was a bit of an anomaly in LA, getting by without a car most of my time there. I managed by riding public transportation and by using these two movable, bendable poles below my waist that I call "legs." People in LA walk for one reason: to get exercise – either for themselves or for their dogs. They never walk to get from Point A to Point B. Now I live in a town that's less than a twenty minute walk north to south. But guess what? Nobody walks here either. On one hand, I think that's a little silly; on the other hand, once I get a car I'm never walking again either.

There are noises. In my former apartment, you could hear the ocean waves lapping against the shore 24 hours a day. In truth, it was the sound of the constant traffic from the 134 freeway, a mere 50 feet from my paper thin bedroom window. After awhile though, the noises all kind of melt into each other and you can convince yourself it sounds like the ocean. Then you hear a screech of tires and a dozen car horns start blaring and your beautiful illusion is shattered. There are noises here, too. Like birds chirping and crickets chirping and other-things-that-chirp chirping. Either the creatures in Los Angeles are mute or I simply couldn't hear them over the noise coming from the freeway.

The water's dirty. That's all I have to say about that.

Small talk is universal. In LA, small talk was always about traffic and the details of how people got from one place to another. In North Dakota, I've found that small talk is usually about the weather, how bad it's been and how much worse it's going to get.

Small talk varies by region; but I think the subject discussed will always be the thing that frustrates people the most in that region. Because whether you live in North Dakota or Los Angeles or Timbuktu, the one thing that makes us all the same is our desire to complain.

Mount Rushmore. (Featuring President Theodore Roosevelt and three other guys.)

This is just one of the many fascinating attractions and educational sites **not** located in North Dakota.

SOMEONE OUGHT TO TEACH A CLASS ON BEING NORTH DAKOTAN

O! Pioneer column originally published 8/22/12

If any of you North Dakota natives are looking for a way to earn a little extra cash, have I got the solution for you! You should teach a class to recent transplants on how to pass as a North Dakotan. This is a class that I would benefit from greatly.

I had been here only a few days the first time I realized that I wasn't fitting in seamlessly. I was with a rather large group at a restaurant. I really wanted the chicken; everyone at my table was ordering the steak. For some reason, I got it into my head that North Dakotans consider steak real food and chicken only ordered by children and sissy boys from the big city. I couldn't shake the mental image of the waitress setting down a chicken dinner in front of me to the shaking of heads and snickering of my companions. So when the waitress asked what I wanted, I panicked and ordered the fish.

No sooner did the meals come than the man sitting next to me said, "You can tell you're from Los Angeles." Aside from the fact that I had just told him this fact, I assumed that the fish had ratted me out. Then he elaborated on his comment, "you ordered fries." Sure enough, every other plate contained either a baked potato or a sweet potato. I was so worried about being judged for my meat selection, I neglected to give any attention to my choice of starch.

That's why I need you to teach a class—to keep me from making embarrassing faux pas like that. (Is using French yet another faux pas?) It wouldn't even take all that much of your time. It could be a once-a-week class, say on Tuesday nights. I'm free Tuesday nights. The first class session could be on waving.

Don't get me wrong: I know how to wave. I learned how to wave at quite an early age. I'm very good at waving, actually. Some might call me a waving virtuoso. But that's the science of waving. What I need to learn is the art of waving.

In Los Angeles, you only wave at the people you know. If that. Here I get waved at by complete strangers! I'll be walking down the street, glance over at a passing car and notice the driver casually lift a hand in greeting. Of course, I do the same. It's actually a pretty good feeling being given this small signal of acknowledgment from someone you don't know.

Then it occurs to me that I haven't really been paying attention to the cars on the street before this moment. Perhaps there has been a steady stream of cars passing me before this, each driver lifting a hand of neighborliness, and I have ignored them. Perhaps in the span of five minutes, I've managed to alienate a large segment of my town and have already developed a reputation as being a snooty big city-er. (Or whatever you call someone who comes from Los Angeles.) Perhaps I'm just moments away from being waved right out of North Dakota.

Paranoid, now I'm walking more slowly, squinting to see into windshields that are obscured by the afternoon sun to see if the driver is waving at me. I'm not noticing where I'm walking. I'm falling down a lot.

Turns out, not everyone waves. And I haven't been able to figure out the pattern. I suppose I could just wave first and wave at everyone; but then what if they don't wave back? My fragile ego couldn't take that.

Now there's a slight chance that I'm over thinking this waving thing. That's why I need you! To tell me when I'm overreacting.

The class wouldn't require much prep time either. You already know how heavy the rain needs to be falling before I can whip out my umbrella and not get strange looks. You already know that soda is called pop and lunch is called dinner. You already know which people I shouldn't talk badly about in front of which other people because it turns out that those people are cousins.

You could call the class "What Would North Dakotans Do?" Every pupil could wear a "WWNDD?" bracelet to remind them between class sessions of all the lessons learned.

You may not get rich teaching this class, but I can guarantee that you'll have at least one pupil. I'll see you Tuesday. Do you accept credit cards?

photos: Jonell Bayer

The Divide County Threshing Bee.

THE THRESHING BEE
from notes dated 8/25/12

I arrived last month just in time for the county's largest annual event: the Threshing Bee. It is put on by the Divide County Historical Society and held the third weekend in July every year. This was the Threshing Bee's 43rd year.

In the month since, I've had several conversations with friends and family over the phone. They all go something like this:

"Have you done anything exciting yet?"

"I went to the Threshing Bee."

"You went where? What?"

"The Threshing Bee."

There is a pause on the other end of the phone. "I don't understand the words that you are saying."

The official name of the event is the Divide County Threshing Show—that's what's written on the official souvenir guide—but everyone I've ever heard talk about it calls it the Threshing Bee. They probably changed it from a bee to a show after enough people complained, "I don't understand the words that you're saying."

"So what is a threshing bee?" you ask. Well, it's just like a spelling bee or a quilting bee, except instead of words or blankets, you have farm equipment.

It takes three days to hold a proper bee. Things started off Friday night (which I missed) with a concert from the Petersons—a large musical family that sings and plays music together. It's like the Partridge Family if the Partridges were also farmers and didn't dress alike. (I assume that the Petersons don't dress alike.)

Saturday is the big event: a parade of tractors! I know that sounds, well, weird; but it's very cool. These are like ancient tractors. Two of them were the original tractors that Noah took on the ark with him (to repopulate the tractor species). It's pretty amazing to see these machines—some of them over a century old—up and running, rolling down the parade route, huge belts turning, sputtering and coughing out carcinogens. You watch them get caught up in a rut on the dirt road and you think, *It's going to stall, it's not going to make it.* And occasionally one does stop dead. But mostly they keep chugging along.

When a tractor does stall, the large crowd collectively holds its breath, willing the thing to start back up again and finish the route. And somehow, you don't know how, all of the tractors make it to the end.

There are non-tractor elements thrown into the parade as well: classic cars (as far back as the Model A), military vehicles, the local fire truck and county sheriff's vehicles, and a few floats from groups like the Sons of Norway. (The Sons of Norway float is the wagon filled with women and children. No men.) But everyone knows the "see" are the tractors.

The parade is 30 minutes of fun and excitement. Unfortunately, the parade lasts an hour and ten minutes. Thirty-five minutes into it, you wish you'd found a shadier place to sit. Forty minutes in, you wonder if the rest of the tractors would be offended if you left now. At the forty-five minute mark, you see a tractor that looks suspiciously like the first tractor and your heart sinks as you consider the possibility that they might be starting the whole parade over again.

Eventually, it ends and then you can get some food at the lunch stand or get a ride on the horse-drawn wagon or see the live threshing demonstration. I could never find where the threshing demonstration was. I saw the horse-drawn wagon at one point but didn't see where it stops to pick up passengers. So I grabbed a pulled beef sandwich at the lunch stand and assumed it would have barbecue sauce. I was mistaken. I sense that I will have quite a few issues with the food in these parts while I'm here.

That evening there is a talent show. That was fun. All musical acts; some of them quite good. It seems like everyone in this area grew up learning how to play an instrument. I feel as if there is more musical talent per capita here than anywhere I've ever lived. Still, I wouldn't have minded a magician or a juggler or a stand-up comedian to break things up a little.

The whole thing is emceed by Rod G., who is a riot. Between acts, he'd tell a joke and then when the audience would laugh, he'd say something like "Oh good, I didn't know if that was funny." You don't know if he's being humble or it's just part of his shtick. Either way, his manner is much funnier than his actual jokes. He's Norwegian through and through.

Sunday morning, there's a church service in a nice little church on the Threshing Bee grounds. The church is only used that one Sunday every year. It was nice. Exuberant singing of a lot of great old hymns—all of which I knew, I think. I sang the melody line, but it seems like the rest of the congregation just fell into four-part harmony. We didn't have the music in front of us, just the lyrics; it's like singing harmony was as easy as breathing. I wish they would have picked up the tempo on some of the hymns though.

After church, there's another parade of tractors for those who missed it the day before or for those who just can't get enough tractor. I was not one of those people.

In the afternoon, there's a big auction. I was already home by that point, so I didn't check it out. But I could hear the auctioneer over the loudspeaker from my house a quarter mile away.

This whole production is held at the Pioneer Village. It's in the southwest corner of Crosby. It looks like, well the name says it all—Pioneer Village. It looks like a village that would have been around during pioneer times. Most of the buildings are ancient, most of them transported here for preservation. There's an old post office from one town, a bank from another town, a terrifying dentist's office from before they invented Novocaine, a shack that a homesteader built so that he would have something to stake his claim on. It's great fun to walk around these buildings and see the instruments and the accessories that accompanied everyday life over a century ago. There was even a blacksmith in a small barn-like building putting on a demonstration.

A newer building serves as the Museum. It stores everything from ancient dolls, to pioneer clothing, to old bicycles. There's some attempt at organizing the material, but not much. A thorough cataloging is more of an undertaking than any of these volunteers signed on for, so the general effect is: "What you see is what you see."

I saw an old picture of a woman in a large hat at Writing Rock. A sign beside it reads, "Do you know who this woman is?" It's not a quiz, they're just hoping that someone will come along someday who can finally identify her. She looked a little bit like Clara Bow—Hollywood's "It" Girl of the 1920s—but that might have just been the sepia tone talking, so I didn't say anything.

And there are vendors around—outside and in some of the buildings— selling their wares. Handcrafted jewelry, collectibles, homemade purses, pictures of cars etched in glass, some old junk labeled "antiques" and some antiques labeled "old junk."

People come to the threshing bee from all over the country. Honestly. There are Canadians here too, but you'd never know it unless they told you; they look just like us!

I just looked it up in the dictionary: apparently "bee" just means a gathering of people for a specific purpose. So that clears up that. Now I just have to figure out what "threshing" means.

IF NOT FOR MY TIME IN MEDORA, I WOULDN'T HAVE THIS COLUMN

O! Pioneer column originally published 9/5/12

POP QUIZ time.

Question 1: Who said that if it weren't for his time in North Dakota he never would have been president?

Pencils down. If you correctly answered "Theodore Roosevelt," then you are either a history buff or you have been to Medora. I took my first trip to Medora recently. In the 30 hours that I was there, I heard no less than 127 times that Teddy Roosevelt credited North Dakota for his presidency. At every attraction, in every shop, on every street corner, they let you know. I suspect they track you somehow to ensure you're getting enough exposure. I imagine a buzzer going off in a control room and a panicked Medoran saying "It's been 15 minutes since John's heard that if it weren't for his time in North Dakota Theodore Roosevelt would have never been president. Quick, send in Amanda!"

I know what you must be thinking. "Wow, John, you went a whole three weeks living and working in North Dakota before going on a vacation. Wherever did you develop such an outstanding work ethic?" To a writer, there's no such thing as a vacation. What you consider a vacation I call "research." (On a side note: Please contact me if you would be interested in financing a two-week research trip to Italy for me.)

I had a great time researching North Dakota's number one tourist destination. In my short time in Medora, I ate steak cooked on a pitchfork, toured a home built by a Frenchman who revolutionized the cattle industry yet still wound up a complete failure, rode in a stagecoach through the Little Missouri Bottom, was waited on by people who wore "Mr. Bubble" T-shirts, and watched the acclaimed Medora Musical. I enjoyed myself very much—a fact which surprises me a little.

(Theodore Roosevelt once said that if it weren't for his time in North Dakota he never would have become president.)

I never had this kind of fun in Los Angeles. The obvious reason is that there is quite a shortage of stagecoaches in LA. The bigger reason however is that Los Angeles is too cool for Medora. Let me explain.

I had a great time at the Medora Musical. The only thing that bothered me were the three pre-teen boys sitting in front of me. At every opportunity they mocked the spectacle going on around them. At the time, I thought these boys were not enjoying themselves at all.

But now I wonder. Perhaps they were trying hard to prove to each other that they weren't having the good time they were really having. They were at that rough stage of life where how others see you defines who you are. You can't be caught "digging" (as the kids say) a group of enthusiastic performers dressed in glittery western attire singing and dancing their hearts out. These boys were too cool for Medora.

(Theodore Roosevelt once said that if it weren't for his time in North Dakota he never would have become president.)

Los Angeles is a lot like those boys. The town is filled with perpetual adolescents who worry about what everyone thinks of them. They are called "hipsters." Hipsters are grown men and women who wear skinny jeans and T-shirts with scarves. They enjoy entertainment ironically—they would call the Medora Musical "kitschy" and make little jokes about it, believing it to be beneath them.

Now I'm no hipster. My "skinny" jeans are the ones that used to fit before I put on some extra pounds. Still I wonder if I don't have some hipster tendencies. I worry too much about what other people think of me. I'm in danger of thinking myself above people who may not have the same background, experiences or education as me.

This is yet another reason that I feel so blessed to be in North Dakota. People seem very straightforward and honest here. I don't get the impression that everyone is looking over their shoulders to see if what they are doing is approved of by the cool kids. I guess you don't have to when you're in a state that the coolest president ever once resided in. By the way did you know that Theodore Roosevelt once said that if weren't for his time in North Dakota...

photo: Jonell Bayer

This gigantic bust of Theodore Roosevelt carved out of butter is located in Watford City, North Dakota.

OK, it's actually stone or concrete or something like that. But it would be a lot cooler if this sculpture was dairy based, don't you think?

THE OUTSIDE WORLD
from notes dated 9/10/12

Last month, I got a taste of how rural and metropolitan communities differ. It was the weekend of the annual Sidewalk Sales along Main Street. (Stop on by! Great deals to be had!) On Friday evening, the Crosby Chamber of Commerce gave away hotdogs and hamburgers in Kulaas Park. They must have fed at least three hundred people. After dinner, the chamber president grabbed a mic and starting listing names of winners in rapid fire. Mine was one of the names called—I had apparently signed up for this somewhere along the way. I went forward to get my prize: an envelope.

I returned to my party, opened the envelope to find two pieces of paper that looked vaguely like Monopoly money. The green one had "20" written on it, the yellow had "5." Or maybe, the other way around.

"What is this?"

They were Crosby Bucks, my table informed me.

Crosby Bucks are redeemable at any business in Crosby. Every single one! I could go into any establishment—even the grocery store—hand them my Crosby Bucks, and the clerk would pretend that I gave them real money and let me walk out the door with their stuff. These strips of yellow and green paper that I could have easily created on the copy machine at work, are legal tender in the northwest corner of North Dakota.

As it so happens, the newspaper where I work is where Crosby Bucks are printed and copied. Though I would never abuse that power. I promise.

That kind of thing wouldn't fly in a big city. In Los Angeles, if you were out walking your dog and someone approached and offered you a copper coin where Marilyn Monroe is heads and Marlon Brando is tails, and said "this counts as $5 anywhere in the greater metropolitan area," you'd say "Nice try, buddy. I don't know what kind of scam you're trying to pull but I wasn't born yesterday." Then you'd take the bag that's gloved over your right hand and pick up the mess your dog left on the grass and continue on your way.

I get the sense that rural communities feel like they're on their own. This allows them to make Crosby Bucks a reality. I think it also binds the people—we're in this together. It borderlines as an *Us versus Them* mentality. There's our community and there's the rest of the world.

For example, no one here cares about the media—except for sports or news. Sure people go to the movies and they watch television; but they don't care about them. In LA, everyone cares very deeply about movies and TV. We're all there because we want to get into the film industry. Most of us were greatly affected and changed by something we saw on the screen. That moment has led us in the pursuit of a dream. It has also given us the misguided impression that everyone is equally as moved by the stories that Hollywood creates. During every conversation you have in LA, you eventually get to talking about the current films out, or you bring up how that person's problem reminds you of that episode of that one show, or you don't know what to say so you just go back and forth reciting your favorite lines from movies.

It's all a bunch of nonsense! None of that means anything here. North Dakota doesn't care about what comes out of Hollywood. Folks around here don't watch anything made after the 1980s—except for news and sports. And *Dr. Quinn, Medicine Woman*, which came out in the 90s. The stories coming from Hollywood today are all about phony, self-absorbed people in big cities who whine their way through life trying to solve self-induced problems living out values that any self-respecting Midwesterner would find appalling. There's nothing there for a real person to care about.

Furthermore, the people I've met don't seem overly interested in what happens "in Washington." There's a lot of political talk, but it's mostly local and state politics. But that might be because I came during a non-presidential election year. I would guess the general feeling is: we live in the one state in the union not experiencing a recession; if Washington just stays out of our hair we'll keep doing what we're doing and be fine.

There isn't really much talk about the 'hot button' issues of the day either: Gay marriage, immigration, the Affordable Health Care Act. I'm sure people have opinions about these things, but we just never discuss them. If it doesn't affect the winter wheat harvest, what's the point in discussing it?

As much as I hate stirring up controversy, I do feel the need to share my stance on immigration. It's not a popular opinion these days, but I believe we should put up a twelve-foot wall along the entire American-Canadian border. I would sure feel safer.

I originally moved to Los Angeles because I had a dream of becoming a sitcom writer. That dream didn't pan out—or at least hasn't yet. I have a lot of problems with LA, but I will give it this: it's a great place to be a dreamer. Dreamers flock to Los Angeles.

When you get on the LA subway—yes, LA has a subway—you are sharing the car with a lot of *going-to-bes*. The man beside you is going to be a famous actor. The woman standing at the front with her bicycle is going to be the next Steven Spielberg. The guy picking his nose across the aisle is going to be the owner of his own film studio someday.

Dreamers are everywhere. We get together and talk about our 'big break' and commiserate about the jobs we have to take to pay the bills until our day comes.

Are there dreamers in North Dakota? I guess so. There have to be, right? But you wouldn't know who they are because we don't discuss dreams here.

At the dinner table, you don't get asked, "Where do you want to be in five years?"; you're asked, "What did you do today?"

You don't say, "I want to write as many novels as Stephen King." You say,

"Guess who I saw at the grocery store?"

You wouldn't even say that you're hoping to save up enough money in a few years so that you and Gladys can see Norway before you die. No, you would save up the money and then tell people that you are going. Or better yet, you wouldn't mention the trip until after you came back from it.

Wishing for something that might not come is impractical. Dreams lack utility, so they aren't worth discussing.

So, it's a trade-off. In rural life, I don't have to deal with all of the B.S. that comes with living in the city. But I also don't get the joy of impracticality.

Then again, I did just purchase a Snickers bar using a slip of canary yellow copy paper. . . . maybe there's hope for this place.

IT'S TIME FOR US TO CONSIDER
THE REAL COST OF THE OIL BOOM

O! Pioneer column originally published 9/19/12

I've been in North Dakota long enough to know there are mixed feelings about the oil boom. There are positives. Our economy is strong (unlike most of the country), once shrinking communities are growing again, and a lot of people who aren't me seem to have a lot of money. There are negatives as well. Every business seems to be short staffed, towns don't have a suitable infrastructure to handle the expansion, and there are some concerns about the potential long-term environmental impact. I've also noticed a few long-time residents seem to resent having to share their town with all of these "oil people."

This is obviously a complicated issue with many facets and points to consider. In all of the discussion about the oil boom, however, we've failed to ask the most important question of all. Namely, how does this affect John Bayer?

The answer may surprise you.

When adventurer George Mallory was asked why he climbed Mount Everest, he famously replied "because it's there." This is a clever and delightfully quotable answer, but it's obviously a lie. George Mallory climbed Mount Everest for the same reason that Lewis and Clark set out on their westward expedition, for the same reason men built the railroads and for the same reason Theodore Roosevelt became president.

The only reason men do anything is to impress women.

When people ask me why I became a writer, I tell them it's because I love to make people laugh. I believe in the power of humor to help people see things differently and to bring them together. This is a fancy way of saying "I write to impress the ladies."

My problem is I can't impress the ladies if I can't meet them. I moved to North Dakota to take on a new environment with new challenges and adventures, which is a fancy way of saying, "I came here to meet girls." But they're not here. Let's face it, for all the extra people this oil boom is bringing to the area, very few of them are single women. (I define "very few" as "none, zero, zilch".)

That's one strike against the oil boom.

Not only is the oil industry failing to bring me eligible women, it's making things worse by bringing in a bunch of other single men that I have to compete with for the affections of the few single ladies there are. And I'm worried I'm not much competition. These guys are in much better physical shape than I am – spending all day moving things and turning things and lifting things. I sit in an office all day and I have the body of a guy who sits in an office all day.

Strike two, oil boom.

Furthermore, I've been led to believe that men who work in the oil field make a lot of money. Don't get me wrong; I earn a decent wage. I want to assure my readers (and the publisher who signs my checks and lets my column run in her paper) I am not complaining about how much money I make. Still, I don't make oil money. Who would a single woman rather be with: a guy who can take her out for steak dinners several nights a week or a guy who makes sure not to buy Pop Tarts until they go on sale?

Strike three. You're out, oil boom. I don't make the rules, I just enforce them. You have two weeks to collect your things and go. I'll be happy to help you pack.

I know with you gone, oil industry, things will be tough around here for a little while; but we'll adjust. We'll make due. We'll get by. And it's not like you can never come back. You are welcome to return to North Dakota as soon as I meet a woman and impress her enough to make her mine. (My parents define "as soon as I meet a woman and impress her enough to make her mine" as "never".)

In conclusion, the oil boom is bad. Very bad. And it must stop. You may disagree with me, and you are more than welcome to your opinion. I'm happy to hear from all of you, whether you agree with me or not. Please send your letters to John Bayer c/o Journal Publishing. And if you are a single lady over the age of 25, please include a recent photo with your letter.

photo: Jonell Bayer

This is something oil-related.

I think.

HOW DO YOU SAY "I'D LIKE A TACO" IN NORTH DAKOTAN?

O! Pioneer column originally published 10/3/12

Being a writer, one of the great benefits of moving to a new region is that one's vocabulary instantly expands. Every region has its own idioms and linguistic eccentricities that have to be learned.

When I first came to North Dakota, I was struck by how obsessed everyone seemed to be with eggs. Here at the newspaper, they talked about the "egg articles" that were going to run in the next edition. In town, people would mention the "egg industry" and even "driving down to the egg."

Honestly, it took a good two weeks for me to realize that you all were actually saying "Ag" and you just didn't have time to bother saying the entire word "agriculture."

I've picked up some words influenced by the area's Scandinavian culture. First, there are the surnames. I love you all, so please don't take offense at this; but your last names are a complete disaster. Too many consonants and not enough vowels, all the letters put together in strange combinations and every other name has at least one letter that's silent. I think you all secretly use name pronunciation as a test—a way to weed out the non-Norwegians among you.

Beyond the name problem though, I've learned a lot. I say "uff da" quite a bit when I'm alone now. One of these days, I'll be confident enough to try it out in public. I know that the red magnets on my refrigerator shaped like horses are Swedish "dala" horses; though I haven't figured out what they're for.

Also I've come to learn who "Ole and Lena" are. It turns out that they're not some couple who live in my neighborhood . . . and if they did, I would probably want to move to a new neighborhood.

The bulk of the North Dakota language, though, seems to be food related. This works out great for me, since my vocabulary was predominantly focused around food to begin with.

I'd already lived in other places that referred to soda as "pop"; but I'd never heard of "slush burgers" until I moved here. Frankly, the name slush burgers sounds very gross to me, not that "sloppy joes" (what the rest of the nation calls them) sounds any more appetizing. I know what lefse is, although I haven't been able to convince anyone to make it for me yet.

I've learned that at a potluck, the word "salad" describes pretty much anything that isn't hot and/or located on the dessert table. And if I'm not mistaken, "hot dish" seems to be a catchall term for any food concoction with meat in it.

By far, my favorite North Dakota phrase is "customer appreciation." Of course, I knew these words long before coming here; but in places like California, customer appreciation means 10 percent off everything in the store. In North Dakota, customer appreciation is defined as "free food at a park or other outdoor venue." (The phrase "grand opening" has the same definition.)

I would have moved to North Dakota years ago if someone would have told me how many free meals I was going to get out of the deal.

By my conservative estimate, in the last two months I have been to at least 47 customer appreciation barbecues. I wasn't even a customer of many of the companies sponsoring these events—but I suppose "customer appreciation BBQ" has a nicer ring to it than "some-dude-who-just-wants-a-free-meal appreciation BBQ." I even ended up being a server at one of these things, somehow; dishing up burgers and hot dogs to the eager masses.

If I have one complaint about all this free food (and you don't have to know me for very long to know that I always have at least one complaint), it's that the "customer appreciation" menu is always the same: burgers and hot dogs. How about appreciating me with a pizza? Or wooing my business with a Mexican buffet? I'm eating five to seven free meals a week here, people. I need some variety.

I know I should just enjoy the free food while it's available. I'm guessing that once the brutal North Dakota winter hits, there won't be a lot of outdoor barbecues for the community.

When I told my friends that I was moving here, everyone warned me about how terrible the winters would be. They all mentioned the cold. Most mentioned the piles and piles of snow. A few told me about the harsh winds. Not one of them warned me that I'd finally have to start buying my own food. Talk about brutal. Uff da!

photo: Jonell Bayer

The pride of Crosby is the Divide County Courthouse at the north end of Main Street.

It's nice.

OLE AND LENA
from notes dated 10/7/12 and 10/10/12

The most famous name to ever come out of North Dakota is probably Lawrence Welk. That sounds like the set-up of a joke, but it's not. This is North Dakota. In North Dakota, we don't joke about Theodore Roosevelt, we don't joke about hail storms in August, and we don't joke about Lawrence Welk.

If you don't watch a lot of PBS, have never been to the Welk Resort in Escondido, California, and are under 80, you may not know who Lawrence Welk was. If that's the case, then the most famous name to ever come out of North Dakota for you is Josh Duhamel. Yep, that's all we've got: Lawrence Welk and the guy who was in the Transformers movie.

We do have two local celebrities, though—folk heroes, really. Their first names are Ole and Lena, but no one seems to know their last name. They're Norwegian, though, so it's probably something like Anderseriksmoendottir.

Ole (pronounced "Oh! Lee") and Lena (pronounced "Lee? Nah!") are the stars of a vast catalog of jokes told by Americans of Scandinavian descent. Ole and Lena are married, although they didn't used to be. One time, during their courting days, Ole was driving the two of them from Dickinson, North Dakota to see Lena's parents in Bismarck. During the drive, Ole placed his hand softly on Lena's bare knee. Lena whispered in

Ole's ear, "You can go fur'der if you vant to." So Ole continued on to Fargo.

Scores of books have been written and published in the Midwest about Ole and Lena. Crosby native, Charlene Power, wrote a series of joke books starring Ole and Lena. And I'm told that back in the day, she had a radio show where she shared the jokes that were sent in to her. There's even a company in Minnesota that makes fortune cookies with short Ole and Lena tales inside them. Like, Ole and Lena stopped at a wishing well. Ole threw his coin in and made a wish. When Lena went to throw her coin in, she lost her balance and fell in. Ole remarked, "Boy, dese tings really vork."

Ole and Lena live in the Midwest. Some people, mostly Minnesotans, claim they're from Minnesota. Ridiculous! The pair are clearly North Dakotans.

Ole and Lena are not the brightest bulbs, but they have a friend, Sven, who is even dumber. Which is to say, Sven is Swedish. Occasionally, other people show up in their lives, namely Hilda and Lars; but I don't know their ethnicity.

I think you can learn a lot about a culture by the jokes it tells. Particularly, the jokes that people tell about themselves. The vast catalog of Ole and Lena jokes reveals what Norwegian-Americans think about themselves, and tells us something of their experiences. Here is a little of what Ole and Lena teach us:

Norwegians like to give off the impression that they're dumb. (Though not as dumb as Swedes.)

• Ole and Sven attend a funeral. Suddenly Ole realizes that he doesn't remember the name of the dearly departed. Ole leans over to Sven and asks: "Sven, do you know who died?" Sven ponders before turning his head toward Ole and says, "I think it vas de guy in de box."

• Ole and Sven returned from a long fishing trip with only one fish to show for their efforts. "The vay I figger it," Ole told Lena upon his return home, "dat one fish cost us $400." "Vell," Lena remarked, "At dat price it's a good ting you didn't catch any more."

Why would a whole people group describe themselves as stupid? I think much of that is born from the immigrant experience—people in a new country who don't quite know how to get along yet. We see a little of that in this joke about technology.

• Ole, Lena, and their son, Little Ole, went to The Cities for the first time. They spent the day walking the busy streets, marveling at the number of people, and admiring the huge buildings. At one point, something caught the eye of Little Ole and he was off like a rocket. He ran into one of the big buildings, with Ole and Lena following close behind. Within the building were two silver doors, the shiniest any of them had ever seen. Just then a fat, mean-looking old hag of a woman came up to the doors. She pressed a button on the wall and the doors slid open. She walked into a tiny room and the doors closed. There was a number 1 above the door and it quickly turned into a 2 and then a 3, 4, 5, 6 and finally 7. A few moments later the numbers went back down until they had gotten back to 1. The shiny doors slid open again. A young, bouncy, beautiful blonde woman strolled out of the tiny room. "Vat kind of machine is dat, Dad?" Little Ole asked. Big Ole replied, "I don't know, son, but push dat button and shove your Ma in dere."

Another reason for the perception of unintelligence stemmed from dealing with the nuances of a new language.

• While on his morning walk, Sven saw a sign in the front yard of Ole's house that read, "Boat For Sale." Now Sven knew that Ole didn't own no boat, no way, so he went in to ask Ole about it. "Hey Ole, I seen dat sign in yer yard," Sven said. "Ya, you looking to buy?" Ole asked. "I got a John Deere tractor and a combine, and dey are boat for sale."

• Lena was competing in a swimming competition—the breast stroke across Lake Sakakawea. Her competitors were a German woman and a Belgian woman. The German woman came in first, the Belgian woman came in a close second. A long time later, Lena finally reached the shore, totally exhausted. "I don't vant to complain," Lena said when she'd had time to catch her breath, "but I tink dose udder two girls used dere arms."

• Lena died in their home, so Ole called 911. The operator assured Ole that she would send someone out right away. "Where do you live?" she inquired. "3500 Eucalyptus Drive," Ole replied. The operator asked, "Can you spell that for me?" There was a long pause. Finally, Ole answered, "How 'bout I drag her over to Oak Street and you pick her up dere?"

Norwegians may play dumb, but at their core, they have an innate ingenuity. Most of the Norwegians I know are tinkerers, problem solvers, fixers. They like to figure out how things work and then come up with ways to make them work better. At times, you can see glimpses of it when Ole and Sven are together.

• Sven was over at Ole's house helping him put up new siding. They had been hard at it for several hours when Ole noticed some strange behavior from Sven. Every so often when Sven would pull a nail out of his apron, instead of hammering it into the siding, he would throw it over his shoulder and onto the ground. Finally, Ole asked, "Ah ya, Sven, vat are you doing dat fer?" Sven replied, "Some of deese nails is broke, Ole. Da head is on da wrong end." Ole just shook his head. "No-No, you dumb Svede, dem nails is fer da udder side of da house."

• Ole and Sven went fishing where they went every summer. This year, though, they decided to rent a boat instead of fishing from the shore. They rowed out into the middle of the lake and caught fish after fish after fish. The little buggers were practically jumping into the boat! Ole said to Sven, "Ve need to figger out a vay to mark dis spot. It's da best fishing I've seen since I vas a boy." Sven replied, "I got some chalk in my tackle box. Vhy don't I put an X right here on da bottom of da boat?" Ole laughed, "You dumb Svede! Dat von't do. Vhat if we rent a diff'rent boat next time?"

Ole and Lena jokes are about more than just intelligence or lack there-of. They also highlight the differences between the sexes—a theme that is universal.

• After church one particular Sunday, Ole was feeling a mite religious. That afternoon, as he swayed away in the hammock in his back yard, Ole looked up to heaven and asked, "God, when you made Lena, vhy did you make her so nice and round and so pleasant to hold?" A voice from heaven called out, "So you would love her, Ole." Not one to be surprised even by the voice of God, Ole then asked, "Vell then vhy, oh vhy, Lord did you make her so stupid?" The voice replied, "So she would love you."

• Ole and Sven were on the lake fishing as was their wont. Ole confided in his friend, "Sven, I tink I'm going to leave Lena." "Oh? vhy is dat Ole?" "Vell Sven, she hasn't talked to me in nearly two months and von't tell me vat I did wrong." Sven considered this, then said, "Ole, I vould tink twice about dis. Women like dat are hard to find."

Also in these jokes, we see an emotional distance, a lack of sentimental-ity—a characteristic that is markedly Norwegian.

• It is the Vikings first home game of the season, and this guy Lars has tickets to the first game. They are in the nosebleed section, but who cares, it's the Vikings. Midway through the first quarter, Lars spies someone he knows through his binoculars. It's Ole, a friend he hasn't seen in twenty years. Ole has amazing seats in front, right on the 50-yard line. There's an empty seat next to Ole—probably the only empty seat in the stadium. Lars keeps an eye on things through the rest of the first quarter and through the second. No one ever comes to claim that empty seat. At halftime, Lars can't stand the suspense any longer. He goes down to where Ole is sitting. After taking a few moments to get reacquainted, Lars asks Ole about the empty seat. Ole says, "My wife Lena, she bought dese seats a long time ago. Sadly, she passed avay." "I'm real sorry to hear dat," says Lars, "but vhy didn't ya give da ticket to a friend or even a relative?" Ole replies, "Tried to. But dey all vent to da funeral."

• This time it's Ole who has died. Lena goes to the local paper to put a notice in the obituaries. The newspaper man offers his condolences before asking what Lena would like the obituary to say. "Ole died," Lena answers. "That's it?" says the newspaper man, "You don't want to say anything else? If you're worried about money, our rates are very reasonable. And the first five words are free." Lena ponders for a moment before speaking. "Ole died. Boat for sale."

• Before his death, Ole spends his last hours at home. The doctor has only given him a matter of hours left to live. While he lies there dying, he catches the scent of his favorite bars wafting through the air. It takes all of his remaining strength, but Ole manages to pull himself out of bed and make his way downstairs to the kitchen. He spies a pan of the delicious bars cooling on the rack. He cuts out a piece for himself and takes a bite of pure heaven. Just then Lena comes in. She smacks Ole on the hand and says, "Shame on you, Ole! Dese are for *after* da funeral!"

In my experience, Norwegians are a generous lot. But Ole and Lena also show us that when it comes to money, wastefulness is to be avoided. Frugality is king.

• One morning, while Lena was doing her sewing, Ole came running into the house. Without a word, he grabbed his wallet and ran back out. Lena followed to see if she could help. Ole stopped at the outhouse, opened the door and dropped a five dollar bill into the hole. Then he took a ten dollar bill out of the wallet and threw that into the hole. "Yumpin' Yiminy!" cried Lena, "vhat are ya doing dat fer?" "I dropped a nickel in der before," replied Ole. "So?" Lena was confused. "So," Ole explained, "I shure ain't going down der for just a nickel."

• Ole and Lena went to a fair. Lena wanted to go for a ride on the helicopter. "Are you kidding?" Ole said, "Ten dollars fer a five minute ride. No vay." Overhearing this, the helicopter pilot said. "Here's what I'll do. I take you both up for ten minutes. If during the flight you don't make any sound, the ride is free. Otherwise, you owe me 10 dollars each." Ole and Lena agreed. During that ten minutes, the helicopter pilot pulled out every trick in the book—quick ascents, twists and twirls, even a loop-da-loop. No sound from the back. As the helicopter touched back to the earth, the pilot commented over the headphones, "Congratulations. You went the whole ride without a peep. I've got to hand it to you." "Tanks, dat vas a close one," said Ole, "I very nearly said something tree minutes in ven Lena fell out."

• It was the first day of ice fishing for the season and Ole and Lena were right there on the lake. When the beer ran out, Lena volunteered to walk across the lake to Sven's General Store and get some more. Ole kindly thanked her and told her to have Sven put it on their bill. "Vhy don't you yust give me da money now?" Lena asked. Ole replied, "Vell, I don't know how tick da ice is."

And finally, you need to poke a little bit of fun at your beloved home state.

• For twenty-five years, Ole and Lena farmed their small plot of land at the bottom edge of North Dakota. One day a surveyor came to Ole and Lena's farm to assess the property. After he was done, the surveyor met with them to deliver some bad news. "I've surveyed your property," he said, "but there's a problem. All of these years you believed your farm was in North Dakota, when in fact you're in South Dakota." Far from being upset, Ole and Lena were almost happy—as close to a Norwegian can get to being happy. "You seem pleased by this news," marveled the surveyor. "Thank you, Yesus," said Ole, "Dis news came yust in time. Lena and I didn't tink ve could handle one more North Dakota vinter!"

Ole and Lena have much more to say, but I will leave them be. After all, I have no interest in telling a bunch of stories about two people from *South* Dakota.

HOW TO SUCCEED IN BUSINESS WITHOUT REALLY TRYING

O! Pioneer column originally published 10/17/12

I might open a donut shop. I could sell freshly prepared donuts and other pastries. Exotic coffees from around the world, too. I don't know of any shop like that in the area, so I think it's a million dollar idea.

In Los Angeles, there's a donut shop on every street corner. With all that competition, each shop has to offer more to stand out.

In my old neighborhood, there was a donut shop that also sold burgers. Another donut shop's menu included fried chicken. My favorite was the combination donut shop/sushi restaurant.

Being in North Dakota, I figure my store could sell donuts in the front and tractors in the back. Or vice versa.

The problem with my plan is that I don't have the money to open a bakery. Also, I like sleeping in and don't want to keep baker's hours. Plus, I don't enjoy baking very much. Aside from that, it would be the perfect business opportunity for me.

I feel like I've got to open some sort of business here. Any business.

I came to rural North Dakota looking for the Pioneer Spirit and what I've discovered is the Entrepreneurial Spirit. In my town of about 1,100 people, 1,075 of them own a business. Even if you work 9 to 5 for someone else, you've got your own thing on the side.

I've always thought that I would be in business for myself someday. I've always been a person of big dreams and huge ambitions; and yet self-employment has never come my way.

So the questions become: Why not? What's missing? What do 90 percent of Dakotans have that I don't?

Dakotans have this innate Entrepreneurial Spirit. But I have that too. There must be more to it.

Dakotans have a strong work ethic. And no wonder: your forefathers left everything they knew and traversed countless miles in harsh conditions to settle a dangerous and untamed land where success wasn't guaranteed. Hard work and determination are in your blood.

In contrast, my father used to walk around our house during Arizona summers wearing only underwear, because it was easier than installing an air conditioner. That seems perfectly reasonable to me—after all, you'd have to get up on the roof and everything.

Dakotans have marketable skills. Ole knows how to build a house, so he opens a construction company. Lena can sew and quilt up a storm, so she sells her wares in her spare time. Sven and Hilda are both great cooks, so they open their own restaurant. Well, I may not be able to do any of those things, but I have talents, too.

Driving. I have a perfect driving record: no tickets, no citations, no accidents. You could hire me to drive you around town or on long trips. As long as I don't have to drive in snow or icy conditions. Also, I don't like driving on interstates, so we'll have to avoid those on longer trips. And we'll have to take your car, I don't have one.

Eating. Are you starting that new diet tomorrow, but you don't have the heart to just throw out an entire pantry full of perfectly good junk food? Don't let it go to waste. Call John Bayer. I'll come to your door—knife and fork in hand—ready to eat you out of house and home. Get on the road to better health today!

Trivia. I'm really good at the board game Trivial Pursuit. Next time you throw a party, you could hire me as your "ringer" board game partner. We'll wipe the floor with your other guests.

I can say the alphabet backwards. I haven't figured out how to turn this into a business yet. If you have any ideas, let me know.

That should be enough to launch "John Bayer, Inc."

Get your checkbooks ready now, North Dakota; the next great business empire is right in your backyard.

photos: Jonell Bayer

Welcome to Crosby, North Dakota. You'll never find any place as "Main Street, USA" as this. If you look closely, you can see Andy and Opie in the background, on their way to the fishin' hole.

Speaking in Norwegian accents.

JEANS DAY
from notes dated 10/27/12

Many businesses in the corporate world have adopted a policy called "Casual Friday." This policy gives employees one day a week where they can dress down. Suit and tie are replaced by polo shirt and jeans. It's a policy designed to boost employee morale while completely confusing customers as to who are the workers and who are the other clients.

I've had several office jobs in my life, but I've never gotten a Casual Friday. My first job was in 1992. I was a senior in high school working part-time for the Pima County Health Department in Arizona. I didn't have to wear a suit, but I always had to have a button up shirt, a tie and dress pants. There was no Casual Friday back then. This was in the day when employers naively believed that receiving two paychecks every month was incentive enough for employees to come into the office and do their jobs.

Before moving to North Dakota, I worked for a television studio in Burbank, California. Now, before you start thinking that sounds glamorous, let me say that I worked in the Contracts Department, on the same floor with the Legal and Business Administration departments. This is as corporate as you can get and still be in the entertainment industry.

We didn't have Casual Friday there either. That's because hardly anyone dressed professionally during the rest of the week. The official company policy was: "Hey! We know you don't want to be here. We don't want to be here either. Just wear whatever the flip you want."

We had one secretary in our department who. . .

(. . . Anyone reading this book who is under the age of twenty may not recognize that word "secretary." That's not a word that's used these days. When I worked for the Pima County Health Department, I was a lowly Clerk. The women above me in the food chain were called Secretaries. In the late 1990s, "Secretary" was deemed a derogatory word—it gave way to Assistant, and was later elevated to Executive Assistant. Sometime around aught six, the-workers-formerly-known-as-secretaries became Administrative Professionals. A Clerk, I believe, is now referred to as the Executive in Charge of Putting Papers in Alphabetical Order. Anyway, back to my story. . .)

. . . At this television studio, we had one Administrative-American who used her wardrobe to let the world know how she was doing that day. If she had found a new love (which happened monthly) she would wear a dress—not a business dress, but a party dress with heels. Her face would be nicely made up and her hair would have that natural look that can only be achieved by working on it for two hours. Between romances, she would be on the hunt, so she'd wear something flirty—like short shorts and a tank top that flattered her store-bought chest. The rest of the time, she would be so depressed that she'd just show up to work in sweatpants and a Lakers jersey, no make-up and frizzy hair pulled back in a sloppy ponytail.

And nobody cared how she dressed!!!

This woman was an extreme example, but she was by no means alone. Why is this behavior tolerated? Because it's "the industry" and we're all artists—even the lawyers and the assistants and the Vice President of Delivering My Mail in the Afternoon. So, it's okay if we can't be bothered to look professional, or put on a clean shirt.

Can you imagine if we'd had a Casual Friday at that place? There'd be people walking around in just a large Hefty bag with holes ripped out for the head and the arms to poke through. There'd be a few dudes in their underwear—"I forgot my Hefty bag."

I'm working in Crosby, North Dakota now and we don't have Casual

Friday here either. We have Jeans Day. Tomorrow is Jeans Day.

Jeans Day is similar to Casual Friday but with two important differences. I'll illustrate these differences with a conversation that happened a long time ago between the two people in town who created Jeans Day. I don't know who they are or when they had this conversation, but I'm fairly sure it happened like this:

"Have you heard about this new thing they're doing in New York? Casual Friday."

"Oh yes, that's when people wear jeans to work every Friday. Why do you ask? I don't see how something happening in New York has anything to do with my life."

"Well, I thought we'd try it out here. It might be fun."

"That would be fun. A lot of fun."

"Hmm. . . we want to have fun, but do we want to have *a lot* of fun?"

"That certainly doesn't sound like North Dakota."

"No, it doesn't."

"I know. How about, instead of wearing jeans every Friday we just do it on the last Friday of every month?"

"That would only be about a fourth of the fun. That sounds about right. We can call it Jeans Day. What's wrong? You look troubled."

"I like that idea, but something's missing."

"I feel that way too. I know what it is. Right now, Jeans Day feels too much like a perk and not enough—"

They say the next part in unison: "—like an obligation."

"You're right, that's what it is. What if workers have to pay a dollar every month for the privilege to wear jeans to work?"

"And we could give the money to different charities?"

"Yeah, or whatever. We can figure that part out later. The important thing is to emphasize that every blessing in life comes at a cost."

Thus, Jeans Day was born. And there was much rejoicing. Well, not *much* rejoicing—just enough rejoicing as the situation warranted.

I'm going to lay out my jeans now, because if I forget them tomorrow, I have to wait a whole month until I can wear them again.

A LETTER TO HEALTHY AND HEARTY NORTH DAKOTANS

O! Pioneer column originally published 11/7/12

Stop looking at me like that. Just stop.

Don't play innocent, you know the look I mean. That look of shock and horror as you see me exiting the post office wearing a parka over top another coat, two sweaters and thermal underwear.

It's a very light parka and you know it. I think you should acknowledge it as such.

And for goodness' sake, please stop asking me that question. You know the question.

It's the one you ask me 10 to 34 times a day: "Are you cold?" Yes, I'm cold! I'm not wearing three pairs of pants at once for religious reasons.

If you must ask "Are you cold?" at least make some attempt to sound concerned for my well-being.

Right now, you sound like you're trying really hard not to laugh. Or worse, you look completely mystified.

You don't seem to realize that it has gotten cold yet and you are thoroughly confused as to why my teeth are chattering. You look as if you've just been given a complicated math problem and your mind is struggling to calculate the square root of snow.

I'm doing my best not to admit that I'm cold; because when I do, you all give me the same sage wisdom: "It's going to get colder." It's a warning. It's as if I'm only allowed a certain number of days a year in which to feel cold and I better not use them all up this early in the season.

As a matter of fact, I'm allowed to be cold as much as I want. I'm cold today. I was cold a month ago. And I fully acknowledge the fact that I will be cold in three months when it's -20 degrees outside (not factoring in the wind chill) and several of my toes have fallen off.

Until that day comes, however, I choose to focus on how cold I am at this moment.

I never really felt like an outsider until the cold came in.

I see you shaking your head at me as I walk past you in the grocery store—me in my full winter regalia, you in a short-sleeve shirt. Or on a really bad day, when the snow is falling and the wind is blowing bitterly and I'm moving gingerly down the sidewalk attempting not to fall flat on my face, while you stroll by in your unzipped windbreaker and smile. I know what that smile means, so just stop it. It means I'm not in your little club.

I remember there being cliques back in high school. We had the jocks, and the goths, and the stoners. Being Arizona, we even had a cowboy clique. I was firmly planted in the nerd clique.

I'm coming to the realization that North Dakota is just one big clique: "The people who can endure a cold, barren wasteland for over half of the year."

Every fall you watch us newcomers with a grin and a gleam in your eye to see whether we have the wherewithal to make it into the club (aka "The Strong") or if we'll have the good sense to hightail it for more hospitable surroundings (aka "The Weak").

So grin and gleam away, North Dakota; I have every intention of sticking it out—shivering and complaining every step of the way.

Besides The Strong and The Weak, there is a third category: "The Snowbird."

Snowbirds are North Dakotans who have shown themselves strong through enough winters to earn a lifetime exemption from ever having to do it again. They are rewarded each year with a six-month vacation to

Tucson.

As someone born and raised in Tucson, I assure you that I'm no stranger to the cold.

We have winter in Arizona, too. Those four hours each year can be quite intense, let me tell you.

Just thinking about it makes me want to put on another ski cap.

photo: Jonell Bayer

Here is the office of The Journal, Divide County's weekly newspaper. This was my place of employment during my time in North Dakota.

That tiny, handsome devil in the picture is me.

That light in the window is the ghost of Sakakawea who haunts The Journal building. . . or it might be the reflection of the camera flash.

ANSWERING QUESTIONS FROM AN OUT-OF-TOWNER

O! Pioneer column originally published 11/21/12

Last month (before the "Snow-maggedon" began), my sister Jonell came to stay with me for a week. She really loved it here. If it weren't for the terrible weather, the insanely high housing costs, and the boxelder bugs; she would probably move here, too.

It was great to have Jonell come. I love my sister and we always have a great time hanging out. Beyond that, I was just excited to have my very first visitor. Here was my chance to share with someone all of the insight and wisdom I have gained since becoming a North Dakotan.

As it turns out, there were plenty of opportunities to educate my sister on North Dakota ways. She had many questions. I, of course, had answers.

Time to eat

"What was that?" she asked.

"What was what?" I asked back.

"That noise."

"What noise?"

"It sounded like an air raid siren," she said. "You didn't hear that?"

"Oh, that. That's the noon siren. It goes off every day at this time."

"Why?"

"Because it's noon." I looked at my sister quizzically. I didn't remember her being this dense.

"But why is there an alarm that goes off every day at noon?"

I stared blankly at my sister. "Because it's noon."

The thrill of the hunt

"Why did you bring me to a hockey rink filled with junk?" she asked.

I gently explained this was an auction and that we were at a hockey rink filled with antiques, collectibles, and memorabilia; not junk. I also let her know that we should be on the lookout for good deals; because if we didn't snag something today there wouldn't be another auction in the area for another four days.

"You all really like your auctions in North Dakota, don't you?"

"It's very practical," I assured her. "It's a quick and lucrative way to get rid of your things in the event you retire or move away or God-forbid pass on."

"Which of those reasons account for this auction?" she asked.

"None. Ole needed to make some room in his house for all of the new stuff he bought at another auction last week."

We left two hours later with eight boxes full of antiques that cost us a total of three and a half dollars. So, all in all, a pretty disappointing outing.

Written in stone

"Why do I have to sign this?" she asked.

"It's customary to sign the guest book when you visit someone." I was getting tired of having to explain every little thing to her.

"We're not visiting 'someone'. This is a rock."

"This is Writing Rock," I corrected her.

I couldn't understand why she didn't want to sign. She'd done it several times on our extended road trip: At a visitors center, at an old abandoned schoolhouse, at the counter of the rental car place.

"You all really like your guest books in North Dakota, don't you?"

"How else are they going to know we were here?" I asked.

"Who's 'they'?" she asked.

"Them."

"Well, I don't care. I'm never signing another guest book."

"Let's change the subject," I begged.

"Fine. Where are we going to church tomorrow?"

"Nowhere, apparently."

You'll have to forgive my sister. She's just not from around here. She's not one of us. Our ways seem strange to her. She doesn't understand how Jell-o can be the main ingredient in a salad. But I still love her.

I'd write more, but the 10 o'clock siren just went off. Time for me to go to bed.

photo: John Bayer

Here's that same picture of my sister again at Writing Rock.

It's a nice picture.

photo: Jonell Bayer

In addition to the two vandalized boulders, Writing Rock Historical Site also boasts a playground.

An old, creeky, 'this location might have been used in a horror film at some point' playground.

ALL THE NEWS THAT FIT TO BE TIED
from notes dated 12/1/12

People in North Dakota love their local newspaper.

I work for *The Journal*, the newspaper for all of Divide County and parts of Burke and Williams Counties. There's been much talk over the past decade about how newspapers are dying. If that's true, no one's informed North Dakota. There are currently 90 newspapers published in a state of less than a million people. Larger cities, like Bismarck, Minot, and Williston, have dailies. Most communities, no matter the size, have a paper that comes out once a week.

The reason community newspapers thrive in North Dakota is that the people can have the best of both worlds. It gives North Dakotans something that is theirs alone—a newspaper covering their neck of the woods, talking about people that they know, informing them of events that they're concerned about, while also serving as a lightning rod on which to focus all of their disdain and criticism.

A local newspaper is definitely greater than the sum of its parts. People love their hometown paper, even as they hate everything about it. The laundry list of complaints against the paper is long:

- It got the facts wrong.
- It got the facts right, but it wasn't information that I wanted aired.
- Yes, you got the quote right—I did say that to you—but I didn't know

you were going to print it!

- Why don't you report more good news?
- Why is there so much fluff (also known as 'good news')?
- Why does my favorite column [*ahem*] only run every other week?
- My aunt subscribed to your paper for 37 years; I don't think we should have to pay to put in her obituary.

(About that last comment, if the newspaper charged only the people who had read it for say two decades or less, we'd bring in about $11.50 a week. The "paper" would consist of some guy standing on the roof of our building and shouting the information to townsfolk.)

People in a small town treat reporters like boxelder bugs—they're not particularly dangerous, but still you'd rather not have them in your home. They get the brunt of the blame for the newspaper's deficiencies. Someone will call the reporter and ask, why didn't you cover this thing that we did last week? The reporter can only reply, "If you had called us last week to tell us it was happening you wouldn't have had to call me this week to complain."

The Journal didn't cover the American Legion baseball season this year. This caused a major stink in certain pockets of the community. When baseball got underway, we were understaffed. (Since this is western North Dakota, we are always understaffed. Like every other business.) There was no way that a reporter would be able to attend each of the games. We asked the coaches to provide us with a roster along with the scores and some highlights (like, who hit the game-winning run) for each game. After several weeks of receiving nothing, asking turned to asking really nicely. "Could you at least send us the scores, so we can report that, pretty please?" People came into *The Journal* to express their feelings about our lack of coverage—"Why don't you cover baseball?" "Why do you only care about football?" "Why do you hate God and America?" At this point we stopped asking nicely and started outright begging—"Please, just write down two numbers. You don't even have to tell us which team is which. We'll just guess."

Nothing. And in the community's eyes, their newspaper failed them.

The point of that story is not to defend the newspaper or chastise the coaches (even though it was all their fault). What I'm saying is this—if you live in a small town and have a burning desire to report the news, whatever you do, don't become a newspaper reporter. Instead take two aspirin, lie down and see if it passes.

If it doesn't pass, get a job at the post office. That's where the real news is anyway. The ladies who work at the post office know everything.

If you get a job as a reporter at a newspaper, you can only write the *facts*. But if you work at the post office, you get to tell the *story*, with all its subtle shadings and deeper meanings. And as a post office reporter you can tailor the news to fit the interests of the person you're talking to. Not like a newspaper, with its "one size fits all" mentality.

I do layout and ad design for the paper, so I get spared most of the vitriol that reporters have to endure. On some level, it might seem strange that I work for the paper, but I'm not a reporter. After all, I am a writer. Or consider myself one, at times.

But the life of a reporter is not for me. For one thing, I have a neurotic, compulsive need to be liked. By everyone. As I have already mentioned, that is not the reporter's fate.

Also, a reporter has to rely heavily on these pesky things called 'facts'. I've found that in my own writing, facts tend to get in the way. I try to use them as sparingly as possible. If I have to associate with a fact, I usually sit on the opposite end of the room and just smile politely as if it were my ninety-three-year-old great aunt who has either gone deaf or senile or both.

That's the other thing: I always try to make a joke out of everything. That could be a hindrance to a reporter. My stories would come out like this: "A representative from FEMA said that the devastation caused by the recent flooding could take decades to repair. Wow! There hasn't been that much devastation around here since Ole Haakenson's second marriage. Am I right?"

A friend in town recently commented that among some people there is a perception that the newspaper was kept in the city council's back pocket—that when a member of local government said "jump," we said "is that on or off the record?"

That is perfect considering that all of our local government officials think we're out to get them.

This is the human subconscious trying to save us from the mundaneness of small town life. There must be more going on. Some sinister workings at the paper—that we're in cahoots with certain organizations, that we're trying to advance a certain political agenda, or that we're on a mission to smear So and So's good name.

Mostly, we're just trying to shave 200 words off this article about the Lutheran Women's Quilting Circle before our Tuesday afternoon deadline, which we could accomplish if we didn't have to answer so many angry phone calls.

Ya, people in North Dakota love their local newspaper.

FALLING FOR NORTH DAKOTA ALL OVER AGAIN THIS WINTER

O! Pioneer column originally published 12/5/12

With all the discouragement and negativity that seems so prevalent in our world today, I think it's important to acknowledge and even celebrate each of life's accomplishments. So this week, I want to take some time to pat myself on the back for my latest achievement.

Namely, I've made it to December without falling down on the ice.

I consider this a major accomplishment. And it is one that I was quite sure I wouldn't reach.

Remember that first snow of the season back in October? I do. I remember my first thought was: "The snow is so beautiful." My second thought was: "Why did I move to a place where it starts snowing in October?"

Later, as I went walking in this winter wonderland—or rather, this early autumn wonderland—my foot slid a little bit on a patch of ice. From the outside it was probably not even perceptible, but I was suddenly hit with a realization: I was going to fall. Maybe not today, maybe not tomorrow, but soon. And probably right on my butt.

So as I continued walking home (shuffling my feet like Tim Conway's old man character on *The Carol Burnett Show*) I repeated this mantra "Don't let it be in October. Don't let it be in October."

And it wasn't in October. And to my great amazement, it wasn't in November either. I don't have quite the same hope for December.

The truth of the matter is, I'm not built for maneuvering on frozen water. In Tucson, Ariz., where I grew up, this wasn't an issue. The only thing I had to worry about was stepping on a rattlesnake, scorpion or an occasional jumping cactus.

I've worn ice skates twice in my life and neither time was I able to move or even remain upright without holding onto something. Clearly, human beings were not designed to balance on two metal blades. At least this human being was not.

So you see, I'm not wondering if I will fall down on the asphalt as I'm crossing Main Street in the middle of the day when there are lots of people around to see it. I know it will happen. What I am wondering is how many times will I fall between now and the spring warm up? (Which I have been led to believe happens some time around the end of June.)

I'm also wondering when will that first fall onto the ice happen? The suspense is killing me. Maybe I should just get it over with.

The best way for me to get the falling down out of the way, I figure, is to take up curling. You might be surprised to learn that I've never curled. (Is that the correct word for it: curled?)

Ten years ago, I doubt I'd even heard of curling. It wasn't a popular pastime in the desert. I don't remember the first time I was told about curling; but I'm pretty confident I didn't believe whoever was telling me about it. "A sport where people sweep ice with a broom? Sure, that sounds like a real thing and not at all made up."

I'm eager to give curling a try. Despite the fact that curling combines my two least favorite things—walking on ice and housework—for some reason it looks like a lot of fun.

So I was very concerned last week when someone told me that they didn't think there was going to be curling in Crosby this year. This will not do.

It seems that with the changing times, some long-held traditions are falling by the wayside. When Tioga lost its Farm Festival, it didn't really affect me. And when Crosby canceled its weekend dedicated to a fermented fish dish, I let it slide. But curling is where I draw the line. (Or sweep the line. Or whatever it is they do in curling.)

We need to keep this tradition alive. If anyone plans to start up curling this year, let me know. I'll be there.

Let's not let curling die. Let me soak up some new life experiences. Let me live some North Dakota traditions. Let me fall on my butt. Repeatedly.

I might as well get it over with.

photo: Gary M. Joraanstad

Despite all the talk of oil, the primary industry in North Dakota is still agriculture. I looked that word up on the internet; it turns out, agriculture is just a fancy way to say 'farming'.

To honor North Dakota's strong agricultural heritage, here's a picture of some sort of farm animal.

INSPECTOR BAYER IS ON THE TRAIL OF A BAFFLING CASE

O! Pioneer column originally published 12/26/12

I've always been a sucker for a good mystery. Whether it's the Father Brown short stories of G. K. Chesterton, the novels of Agatha Christie or the movies of Alfred Hitchcock, I can't get enough. I'll even watch an old episode of *Murder, She Wrote* if I'm desperate.

Coming to North Dakota has made me feel like a detective. Just call me Inspector Bayer.

There are many cases on the Prairie for Inspector Bayer to solve. There are historic cases (The Mysterious Stones at Writing Rock), and cultural cases (The Case of the Norwegians Who Eat Lutefisk Even Though They All Agree It Tastes Awful). Then there are the mysteries that only I seem to care at all about, like The Case of the Unexplained Noontime Siren.

All of these mysteries have been put on the back burner in favor of Inspector Bayer's latest intrigue: The Case of the Man Who Moved to North Dakota and Immediately Gained Twenty Pounds.

It's a baffling case. This particular man—for the sake of anonymity, let's call him "I"—was born in Arizona but has lived in Indiana, Virginia, and California. Each time I moved to one of these other states, I lost about 15 or 20 pounds. This was also an unexplained phenomenon, but I never had any real desire to solve that case.

One clue as to why I've gained all this extra girth is that no one here seems to care what I weigh. I moved here from Los Angeles, where celebrities are now sold by the pound, so movie studios are constantly trying to get them to "just drop five more." Even if you're not famous, there is constant pressure in Los Angeles to look emaciated, weak and waif-like; and the women have it rough too.

But in North Dakota, it's different. There are plenty of people in good shape here, but no one seems to care that I'm not. In fact, just the opposite it true.

When I complain to someone here that I've gained weight, they tell me that I'm supposed to pack on the pounds to get through the winter. Apparently they're under the impression that I will soon be heading into a cave somewhere and sleeping for two straight months. Although that sounds lovely and seems to work fine for the grizzly bear, I have to hold down a job. I have rent to pay.

Of course that job involves a lot of sitting. My major form of exercise at work is opening my mail. That, and walking three doors down to the convenience store to buy another candy bar.

The mystery of the extra weight becomes more perplexing when you consider the fact that I've joined a gym. Some people might think that joining a gym would help stem the tide of weight gain and possibly even help me get into better shape. Some other people might believe that joining a gym isn't enough; that I have to actually go to the gym in order to reap the health benefits.

I may not go to the gym very often, but I still get in two workouts a day. There's the half hour routine in the morning, where I put on my winter clothes. Then there's another workout at the end of the day, when I remove my winter clothes.

When I'm not working, I try to stay active during the day. I really do. It's the night that gets me, though. When nighttime comes, all I want to do is curl up in front of the television and snack. Currently nighttime in North Dakota begins at 4:30 in the afternoon and ends around 9 the next morning. This means I spend a lot of time these days eating and watching old episodes of "Murder, She Wrote."

This brings the inspector to the next clue: Food. Again, this seems to be a dead end. I thought when I moved to a town that didn't have a McDonald's, that I would be losing weight left and right. Not so.

I mostly eat at home; and I think I eat responsibly. I'm not perfect. Most mornings, I'm in a rush and miss "the most important meal of the day." But I make up for it in the evening by eating three dinners. Also I try to avoid eating the empty calories that some foods—like vegetables—provide.

I'm stumped. The Case of the Man Who Moved to North Dakota and Immediately Gained Twenty Pounds has proved to be a perplexing one. I don't have the answers now, but Inspector Bayer has never given up on a case.

I know, I know; I should stop complaining. I've got it good. I'm happy and (relatively) healthy. I have good friends and a family that loves me. And I have just enough time to finish off this bag of potato chips and watch one more episode of *Murder, She Wrote* before the sun comes up.

photo: Gary M. Joraanstad

Many people don't realize that North Dakota leads the country in the production of abandoned wooden buldings in the middle of nowhere.

The majority of these structures also lean, which adds to their value.

WHAT'S IN A NAME?
PART I
from notes dated 1/7/13

At one time, "John" was the most popular name in the world. I don't know when that was, but my mother said this to me as a child, so I know that it's true. It's certainly a popular name in the Bayer family. My grandfather was John Bayer. His brother—my great uncle—is also John Bayer. (It's a long story!) Since these brothers had the same first name, my great uncle grew up being called by his middle name, Peter.

My dad is a John. Since his dad was a John also, my dad grew up being called Jack, which some sick soul decided long ago was 'short' for John. Friends of JFK called him Jack. The infamous Jack the Ripper was actually born John Rippenstein.

I, obviously, am also named John. In keeping with the family tradition of not calling people by their given names, I went by "Kris" as a child—in honor of country music legend, Kris Kristopherson. Also, it's my middle name.

My dad's brother is, strangely enough, not named John. He is Tony. However, he and his wife, Flo, named their son John. They were unaware that Kris was really John Kristopher, and they thought it would be a shame that such a great name would not carry on in our family.

So, in the Bayer clan, we have Johns to spare. In the outside world, though, Johns aren't such a common occurrence. There were no Johns at church. There were no Johns at school. I started going by my first name in the third grade in order to stand out from all the other boys named "Kris" and "Chris". Sure, every so often you'd hear about a disgraced politician or a shady televangelist named John Something. But that was about it.

"Wow John, that's a great story," you're probably thinking, "Thanks for sharing all of that which had absolutely nothing to do with North Dakota whatsoever."

I do have a point. And it's this: In North Dakota, there are still men named John. I'm not talking about Jonathan or, God help us, Jon. I'm talking about the real deal: J-O-H-N.

John is a good solid, salt-of-the-earth type name. And over in good solid, salt-of-the-earth North Dakota, it's a name that's still used along with names like Marlin, Verner and Knute, which proves that parents were giving their children cruel names long before Gwyneth Paltrow named her daughter Apple.

I worked with another John at the newspaper. This John used to own the paper and still works there without receiving a paycheck because newspapering is in his blood and because he likes to keep busy. On his down time, he's a Senator in the North Dakota state legislature.

In contrast, I used to eat cold Pop Tarts at work because I couldn't muster up the energy to walk all the way to the back where the toaster was.

People do not confuse me with the other John at work.

Another John in town loads the projector at the movie theatre. He is also a farmer and participates in just about every civic and charitable organization in town, although he doesn't lead Boy Scouts anymore. I guess after 30 years, he decided it just wasn't for him.

Similarly, to keep busy, I've watched all ninety-three episodes of the 80s sitcom Soap...in order.

There are many other Johns in Divide County, all of them hardworking North Dakotans. Each of them a better man than me. I could list them all, but it would get too depressing. The whole point is. . . hmm. . . it seems like I would have had a point to make after all of that.

I guess I'm just lamenting the fact that John is an endangered species—on the way out. But I'm glad that, at least for now, there's still a place in this world where a group of guys can get together and just be John.

photos: Jonell Bayer

These are the grain elevators. They are located in the center of Crosby.

That is the extent of my knowledge about grain elevators.

NEXT TIME I LEAVE THE STATE, I MAY JUST WALK

O! Pioneer column originally published 1/16/13

People move to North Dakota for a variety of reasons. Some come for the job opportunities. Others might move here to be close to family and friends. Before the oil boom, I'm sure there were people who came because North Dakota had a low cost of living. I myself moved here looking for adventure.

(There's some question as to how successful I've been in that pursuit. It turns out that I'm not much of an adventurer. Most days, I just veg in front of the TV, praying for the spring thaw. I should probably change the name of the column from "O! Pioneer" to "O! Guy-who-just-writes-to-complain-about-the-weather".)

Whatever reasons bring people to North Dakota, there has to be something else that compels them to stay. As you know, not everyone stays. Most oil patch laborers work insanely strenuous hours for a year or two, pack up their big bags of money and head back to their "real" homes. Other folks find the winters just too difficult to bear, and choose not to stay. ("There he goes complaining about the weather again.")

For the people who do choose to live here, year in and year out, what is it that compels them to stay? The answer, I believe, is this:

Laziness.

It's not that we don't all want to leave. It's just that for most of us, it's way too much hassle.

I stumbled upon this pearl of wisdom last month, while waiting at the Minot airport for my much anticipated vacation to begin.

For those of you unfamiliar with the Minot airport, it's small. About half the size of the condo I'm renting. This may have been plenty of room a few years ago; but it's not these days. Five or six airlines share two gates, TSA security eats up much of what used to be the passenger waiting area, and baggage claim is located in a janitor's closet in the back.

The personnel are overworked and understaffed, and it shows in their attitudes. Being in the Minot airport is reminiscent of my time at the Los Angeles DMV.

My trip had been a logistical nightmare from the beginning. Since I don't own a vehicle, I had to find rides both to and from the airport. Luckily, two of my coworkers would be driving through Minot on their way to Minnesota and they let me hitch a ride with them. But they were leaving the day before I flew out, so I had to rent a hotel room for the night – a flea trap within walking distance of the airport.

The day of my flight, as I walked from my hotel to the airport, it was snowing—lightly but steadily. I worried that planes may not be taking off. I arrived to find that planes were still flying, but they were delayed by hours. At the gate, I sat next to one family whose flight had been repeatedly delayed. They had boarded and de-boarded the plane twice already. Their 6:45 morning flight finally took off around 12:30 in the afternoon.

So, yes, the weather was slowing things down, but planes were still taking off. Save for one. My plane. After waiting six hours, we were finally informed that our flight was canceled. A mechanical issue had grounded our plane and the mechanics in Minot couldn't fix it. The airline would have to fly a mechanic in from Vegas. Hopefully, he could get it fixed and we would be able to fly out the next day. My three-and-a-half day trip was now a two-and-a-half day trip.

During the two hours I waited in line for a hotel room voucher, I gave serious thought to canceling my Arizona vacation. If I'd had a car, I probably would have driven back home and hidden under the covers of my bed, only coming up for air around Groundhog Day to find out if I saw my own shadow.

Thankfully, my flight did leave the next day—after a two-hour "deicing" —and I had a great time visiting with my parents and sister.

The week leading up to this trip, my boss told me several times that I "had better make sure I came back." At the time I thought she was making jokes, but now I realize the truth. It's just so hard to get out of this state that once you do it successfully, you question whether you want to ever have to do it again.

My guess is that the Norwegians who first came here weren't really looking to settle in a place as cold and unyielding as the homeland they had just left but after having done it once, they simply didn't have the energy to go through it again.

And I bet Lewis and Clark would still be stuck in North Dakota if Sakakawea hadn't shown up to say "Okay fellas, let's move it along."

So, I'm here. I'm glad to be back. I have no future trips planned. It's too exhausting to think about. I may never leave again.

photo: Gary M. Joraanstad

Just in case you forgot that you were in North Dakota, this sign is here to remind you.

Zero degrees at 9:33 in the morning—worst Fourth of July ever!

THERE'S NOTHING TO DO
from notes dated 1/20/13

It's 9:30 on a Tuesday night. I'm restless and looking for something to do. I consider my options—watch more television or go to bed.

I'm definitely not going out. It's January. There's a foot of snow on the ground and I have no car. None of that matters, since there's nowhere to go anyway.

There's a stereotype about small towns—that they roll up the sidewalks as soon as the sun goes down. But this far north, the sun goes down at a quarter till five in the winter and after ten in the summer. For the sake of consistency, they just close everything at 9 around here.

The "rolling up the sidewalks" imagery doesn't really work around here either. Aside from Main Street, there isn't much in the way of sidewalks. Sidewalks encourage walking. Walking could lead to strolling, which could eventually lead to dancing, which is just a stone's throw away from gambling, stealing and all kinds of debauchery. It's safer just to drive.

In Los Angeles, you can go grocery shopping at 3:00 a.m. I know—I've done it. Down the street from where I used to live, there's a diner that never closes. Even the Kinko's nearby stays open until midnight.

In Crosby, our grocery store closes at 7 p.m. on Mondays, Wednesdays, Thursdays and Saturdays but stays open until 8 p.m. on Tuesdays and Fridays. It's closed on Sundays. Of the four restaurants in town, I believe one is open until 9, one until 8 and the other two just lock up whenever the staff get restless. Our "Kinko's" is the newspaper where I work, and we're out the door at 5:30 every afternoon.

One of the television stations, out of Minot or Bismarck, still signs off at the end of the day. That's something I haven't seen happen since I was a kid.

It's an adjustment!

To be fair, not everything is closed right now. The bars are open. There are two bars on Main Street. At the steakhouse, the kitchen is closed, but I'm sure the lounge is still open for those who want some booze. The Moose Lodge also serves up liquid refreshments, but I'm not sure when they're open or for how long—they might be open now.

I'm not much of a drinker though. I've never had much of a taste for alcohol. I could go to the bar and get a Sprite, but I don't really want to be *that* guy.

On a side note, the two bars in town are right across the street from one another on Main Street. There are two gyms in town, on First Avenue North, also right across the street from each other. Our two auto supply shops are also right across the street from each other. I think the only reason this town only has one grocery store is because the lot across the street from the current grocery store isn't for sale.

I guess small towns aren't very recreation-minded as a rule. You can go to the movies during the weekend. You can join one of the fraternal organizations—the Moose, the Sons of Norway, and the Lions Club. And you can drink.

There's a railroad track that cuts Crosby in two. Where Main Street and the railroad tracks intersect, there are huge grain elevators that store the crops until they are sent out to feed the good people of America. Or to feed the livestock of America. Or the people and/or livestock of some other country. Look, I'm not really sure where the crops go, okay?

Regardless, farming is the center of this town—both symbolically and literally. And farmers are not known for partying.

In Los Angeles, there is no center of town. This is also symbolic. There's no focus, no purpose in Los Angeles. So recreation abounds. Half the people in that city don't have a job, but they can spend the money they don't have to go bowling at 1:30 in the morning.

Ah, what I wouldn't give for a bowling alley about now! Years ago, there was a bowling alley in town. The building is still there. I'm not sure why it closed, but I would venture to guess it was because North Dakotans found it too impractical. "You're telling me I'm supposed to roll this ball from all the way back here and knock down those pins? I could just walk down there and kick them over. It would be a lot more efficient."

Sports may be the only truly accepted form of recreation in these parts—high school sports like volleyball, hockey, basketball, baseball, football. Especially football.

American small towns in general have a reputation for being football-focused. In Indiana, high school football is an obsession. In Texas, it's a religion. In North Dakota, it's not a bad way to spend your Saturday provided you've got all your seeding done.

Don't get me wrong, North Dakotans love football, but they have a hard time showing their emotions. They wouldn't want football to get the wrong idea.

People come to the high school football games in droves. It's the largest assemblage of townspeople you'll ever see outside of a threshing bee. But where Indiana crowds cheer like mad and Texas crowds just start shooting their guns in the air, North Dakota fans are pretty subdued. They'll call out "First Down" when prompted by the announcer until they get tired of it halfway through the first quarter. And they'll clap judiciously when the home team scores. And they'll say to themselves "well now, that's a shame" when there's a turnover. But mostly it's just thoughtful, silent watching. As if the crowd thinks the football game might break out into a round of golf at any moment. That is, until. . .

The post season! The Divide County Maroons ("*WE ARE DC!*") had an undefeated season this year, so they had the luxury of playing their entire post season at home, which meant I got to attend every game. And let me tell you in that week between the end of the regular season and the start of post, something happened to these people.

I think the pressure and excitement finally overtook them and they just collectively snapped. They turned wild, feral—replacing the golf claps with yelling and standing and cheering. It was behavior unbecoming a Norwegian, I'll tell you that much.

Maybe we've had such a good football team for so long that the regular season no longer really matters to them. Or maybe by the post season, it's gotten so cold that everyone has to jump up and hoot and holler to keep from freezing to death. Whatever the reason, I've never seen people around here act this way. It's exciting. And a little frightening.

By the way, it was a glorious post season for Divide County. Some nail biters but we continued our winning streak and made it all the way to the state championship in Grand Forks. The team that wasn't us took the title. It was a disappointing loss of course, but an absolutely great year for the team—and the community. And in some miniscule way, I was a part of it.

It's a great place to be a part of, even if I can't go to the grocery store to buy Pop Tarts at 10:30 p.m.

ACTIVITIES TO WHILE AWAY
A COLD WINTER'S DAY

O! Pioneer column originally published 1/30/13

I'm a writer. Since people tend to attract like-minded people, I have more than a few friends who are also writers. When we exchange emails or talk on the phone, invariably the topic of our work comes up.

"What are you writing these days?" my friends ask.

"Well, I write a bi-weekly humor column," I reply.

Then comes the pause. The pause says: "But aren't you doing any real writing?"

I don't like the pause. The pause makes me uncomfortable. So I add, "I also have an idea for a book set in the town where I live."

My friends get excited with this news. What I don't tell them is that I've had this idea for months and haven't written anything yet.

"You should definitely write a book," they tell me. Then they always add, without fail, "It's the perfect way to spend that long North Dakota winter."

They're right. I know they're right. It's cold outside; way too cold to go anywhere. Especially without a car. I rarely leave my house – other than work and grocery shopping.

It's as if North Dakota herself is telling me: "You should write your book."

And she's right. I know she's right.

But I know something else. I am a writer. And like all writers, my primary goal on any given day is to do everything I can to avoid having to sit down and actually write.

And I'm quite good at avoiding writing. I've elevated avoidance to an art form.

So I thought that I would share with you some of my expert advice. You may not be avoiding work, but you still have to get through this long, cold season just like me. We're all suffering this winter wonderland together.

Here are some of my tips for spending a cold winter's day:

Take part in a marathon. Several friends of mine in Los Angeles competed in a half-marathon a couple of weeks ago. And while you can't go run a marathon outside—at least not without losing a few toes – you could still get into shape. Drag that treadmill out of the garage and start running a virtual marathon. For the less-athletically inclined, like me, you could settle for watching a Law & Order marathon on the USA Network.

Play a board game. This is a great way for a family to not only while away the hours but it's also a chance to deepen your connection to each other.

When you live alone, playing a board game against yourself doesn't hold quite the same thrill; but it still kills some time. Also, you get a little exercise from continually getting up and walking to the opposite side of the Scrabble table. If you do live alone, be aware that playing certain games by yourself is just downright sad. Twister, for instance.

Listen to music. Just remember that when you blast your stereo, you don't want it so noisy that it disturbs the neighbors; but it should still be loud enough to drown out the sound of your heavy sobbing caused by the fact that you've been trapped inside your house for 12 days straight.

Take up a hobby. The Internet can be a great tool here. You could watch an online video to learn to sew. You could find a how-to site that teaches you woodworking skills. Or you could go to a medical site like WebMD, type in the slightest symptom you have and then imagine that you suffer from all the horrific conditions that the website suggests. Hypochondria is great for killing a few hours.

Clean. If you get really desperate for something to do, you could always give your house or apartment a thorough cleaning. I have never been this desperate.

Read. Go to the library and check out a few good books. Or read again some of your old favorites that are on your own shelf.

Or do what I do. Pull out past editions of the newspaper and read the old *O! Pioneer* columns. I can spend hours, reading and laughing, then rereading and re-laughing. Each time is like reading it for the first time.

As I wipe the tears of joy from my eyes, I think, "That guy should write a book."

photo: Gary M. Joraanstad

In North Dakota, you often have to share the highway with slow-moving farm vehicles.

Fortunately, vehicles like this one are so high off the ground that you can just drive under them. No problem!*

*Problem! Do not attempt. Professional driver on a closed course.

Author's Note: Gentle reader, sometimes life is hard.

You have a busy week. Family dynamics becomes stressful and strained. You encounter a teensy-weensy little bout of crippling depression. When these things happen, sometimes you just have to make your life easier. You eat out instead of cooking or you half-ass it at work. No one can blame you for "phoning it in."

That's what I did on February 13, 2013. I phoned it in. I don't remember what was happening at the time, but for whatever reason I didn't get around to writing an original column. So, I plagiarized myself – from a blog I used to write – and passed it off on the poor people of North Dakota.

It's not a terrible column. In fact, at certain points it borders on being funny. It just doesn't have anything to do with North Dakota or life in a small town or anything that my column was supposed to be about.

I've included it here because I wanted the book to contain all of my columns as they first appeared. But you have my permission to skip over this one if you like. I won't be offended.

I'm sorry. It won't happen again.

THE SINGLE PERSON'S GUIDE TO SURVIVING VALENTINE'S DAY

O! Pioneer column originally published 2/13/13

Before I moved to North Dakota, I used to write a blog. For those of you who don't know what that is: a blog is sort of like a newspaper column. But instead of being in the newspaper where only a few hundred or a few thousand people read it, the blog is on the Internet where millions can read it. Unfortunately, everyone on the Internet is so busy looking at pictures of kittens that look vaguely like celebrities or writing their own blog, that no one bothers to read your blog. If you want people to read your stuff, you're better off getting your own newspaper column like me.

My blog was called "John Tells You How to Live." It was the world's best advice column. Unless, you actually followed the advice; then it was terrible.

(If you're crazy bored, feel free to check it out at johntellsyouhowtolive. wordpress.com.)

Last year, I wrote a column with advice for single people on how to survive the most dreaded of holidays—Valentine's Day. It was (I think) a pretty funny piece, so I thought it was worth reprinting it here. Or maybe, I was just too busy not getting dates that I didn't have time to write anything new. Either way, here's the column:

Valentine's Day is just around the corner. Many people celebrate this most sacred of holidays by bingeing on chocolate, crawling into a hole and wishing that they were dead. These people are called 'singles.' Singles have long been ridiculed, pitied or outright mocked on Valentine's Day. And rightfully so!

But times are changing. In our current climate of political-correctness and inclusiveness, the notion that Valentine's Day is strictly a day for couples has become antiquated. Despite the cultural climate change, most singles are still at a loss as to how to spend Valentine's Day. Fear not, lonely loser; I am here to help!

There are plenty of activities that singles can do this Valentine's Day. Here are just a few:

Cry. This is a very popular option.

Catch up on your sleep. You sure as heck aren't going to a nice restaurant or to a movie tonight. Why not get a few extra *zzz*'s? You might also consider multitasking by combining these first two activities: Cry yourself to sleep.

Finally track down the source of that strange smell coming from your kitchen. It's getting worse.

Throw a birthday party for Arizona. Arizona—my home state—became the 48th state on February 14, 1912. Why not have a party (with other single losers) to acknowledge that fact?

Cook a lovely dinner for two. Just because there's only one of you, doesn't mean you should have to settle for a pathetic single portion dinner from the freezer section of the grocery store. Lovingly fix a larger meal from scratch. Eat half of it with a nice glass of wine. Refrigerate the other half of the meal for your next day's lunch. Watch some sappy romantic movie on Lifetime. Finish off the bottle of wine. Consider the distinct possibility that you will die alone. Take the other half of dinner out of the refrigerator and eat it. Drink another bottle of wine.

Send yourself flowers at work. Go ahead and treat yourself. Why should your coworkers who actually have people in their lives that care about them have all the fun? Have a dozen roses sent to the office from someone named 'Paul' (or 'Paula', depending on how you swing). The danger here is that your coworkers are likely to say to themselves, to each other, or to you: "I've never heard Marge mention a 'Paul.' I bet she sent them to herself. How pathetic." (In this scenario, I am assuming that your name is Marge. Or at the very least, your coworkers call you Marge.) To avoid this outcome, I recommend sending yourself five different bouquets throughout the day, all from different suitors. Your coworkers would never suspect you of being pathetic enough to fake five admirers. Well, you showed them!

Get drunk. Tongue-numbing, memory-erasing, fall-down drunk. Do this at home, of course. Going out alone is anathema on Valentine's Day. It's almost always a good idea to get drunk whenever life isn't going your way; but it's especially a good idea to do it on Valentine's Day. Particularly if you own a cat. That way, when your coworkers ask you the next day, "What did you do last night?" you can honestly answer, "I got so drunk, I really have no idea. All I can tell you is that I did not wake up alone this morning."

There you have it. Plenty of options for spending your Valentine's Day alone. It's your day too, single. Make the most of it!

photo: Gary M. Joraanstad

A field of sunflowers in Winter.

Mother Nature's way of reminding us that love is fleeting and everything beautiful dies in the end.

FINDING A COMEDIC VOICE
EVERYBODY CAN APPRECIATE
O! Pioneer column originally published 2/27/13

For me, the greatest joy of moving to North Dakota has been writing this column. I've always loved putting words together in a such a way that it makes people laugh. And through *O! Pioneer* I've been able to do that on a regular basis.

Just about every week, someone I don't know comes up to me and tells me that they enjoy the column. From time to time, people even write to the newspaper to share their appreciation. I want to extend my thanks to each of you. It means the world to me.

At the same time, I realize that comedy (like all art) is subjective. For every person that loves my skewed, sarcastic take on North Dakota and my place in it, there's probably at least one other person who just thinks I'm a jerk.

I'm not everyone's cup of tea. I was reminded of this a couple weeks ago, when someone came up to me and asked: "Do you really think everyone in North Dakota is lazy?"

She was referring to a previous column where I wrote about my difficulty in getting away on vacation due to a combination of bad weather and a ridiculously difficult airport experience. I came to the joke-y conclusion that the only reason people stay in the state is laziness.

This person may have found my column laughable, but I could tell she didn't find it funny.

The irony is that from my experience North Dakotans are some of the hardest working people that I've ever met. Also, I've found that in general they have a strongly self-deprecating humor, which I love. But that was not the case this time.

I need to get over it. Abraham Lincoln said that you can't please all of the people all of the time. That is certainly true about comedy. The problem is that I want everyone to like me. Strike that, I need everyone to like me. So as Theodore Roosevelt said: "If you need something bad enough, you'll find a way to make it happen." [Editor's note: Theodore Roosevelt did not say that.]

In the spirit of getting everyone to like me, I've decided to cast a wider comedy net. The cynical sarcasm that might turn off some will be giving way to a friendlier, more approachable brand of humor.

I've decided to emulate Jeff Foxworthy. He's been a successful comedian for decades, he has a huge fan base, and no one doesn't like him.

He's the guy who tells those "you-might-be-a-redneck" jokes. Here's one of his: "If you think 'loading the dishwasher' means getting your wife drunk. . . you might be a redneck." See? Fun for the whole family!

Now I don't know too much about rednecks, but I have been in North Dakota long enough to learn a few things about Norwegians. So for all of my fans—current and soon-to-be—I present my first batch of you-might-be-a-Norwegian jokes. Enjoy!

If you complain about the heat once the thermometer hits 52 . . . you might be a Norwegian.

If you personally know more than two men named "Knute". . . you might be a Norwegian.

If you refuse to eat Swedish cuisine because it's "just too dern spicy". . . you might be a Norwegian.

If your last name contains twenty-three consonants and no vowels. . . you might be a Norwegian.

If you believe that all men are created equal; but Lutherans are just a little more equal than everybody else. . . you might be a Norwegian.

If you haven't ever told your wife of 30 years about the metal plate in your head you got during the war because "I'm not one to complain". . . you might be a Norwegian.

If you feel the slightest bit guilty that you've only kept seven jobs since you hit retirement age. . . you might be a Norwegian. [See? See, I don't think you're lazy.]

If you can't bring a salad to the church potluck because there's no Jell-o or mayonnaise in the house. . . you might be a Norwegian.

If you're not one to engage in PDA (public displays of affection) with your spouse, you might just be modest. But if your definition of "PDA" includes smiling, making eye contact or calling your spouse by name. . . you might be a Norwegian.

If the rowdiest football fan you have is that guy who clapped twice during the playoff game. . . you might be a Norwegian.

There you have it. So, does everybody like me now?

No? That's OK, I can come up with something better. Um, let's see. "Knock, knock. . ."

photo: Jonell Bayer

A photograph of a North Dakota field in Springtime.

Unfortunately, this photo is in black and white, so it doesn't begin to capture the true beauty of this landscape.

Here is a photograph of that same field in Autumn.

This photo **is** in color.

WHAT'S IN A NAME?
PART II
from notes dated 3/11/13

One in three high school girls in North Dakota is named MacKenzie. Here at the newspaper, we cover everything that happens at the local school: Social activities, high school sports, and in few months graduation and prom. No matter what the event, if it's happening at the high school, guaranteed there will be at least two MacKenzies in the mix. Sure, they're all spelled differently—Makenzie or Makynzie or just Kinzi—but it's still the same name.

I don't know if this is a national epidemic or just a North Dakota thing, but it has to stop!

Now I have nothing against the name MuhKinZee. In fact, it's very lovely.

But does everybody have to be named Maakhensee? There are plenty of other perfectly nice names out there.

Let's introduce some new names into the mix—like Evelyn and Mildred and Audrey. These used to be old lady names, but I feel like they've been out of circulation long enough and would now be considered funky and quirky. Funky and quirky are the two major considerations for today's parents when naming a child.

Mabel and Agnes are ready to make a comeback too. I can see it now:

Teenage boy places a call on his cell phone. After a couple of rings, a sweet young lady answers.

HER: Hello.

HIM: (awkwardly) Um, hey there. Would you like to go out with me on Friday night, Eunice?

HER: Oh, I would love to, Torch. But could we make it Saturday? Friday, I'm supposed to visit my great aunt MacKenzie in the home.

LET ME TAKE YOU ON A JOURNEY
TO A MAGICAL LAND

O! Pioneer column originally published 3/13/13

As I sit at home writing this column, winter is entering its fourteenth month in North Dakota. But I'm not complaining (for once). I look out my window at the unending canvas of snow and I consider what an exotic location western North Dakota has turned out to be for me. Truly.

Most of my friends are more well-traveled than me. Some have taken honeymoons in Europe, others have gone on mission trips to Africa, still others have taken employment in Asia. I, on the other hand, have never even been out of the country.

At least that was the case before I moved here.

Being a desert dweller from birth, the reality that people lived this far north always struck me as odd. Or even sacrilegious. You see, I've always secretly believed that a frozen, unyielding wintery climate was God's way of saying "You shouldn't be here." Not being one to go against the wishes of the Almighty, my plan was to stay in warmer climes.

But now I live in North Dakota, at the northern edge of civilization. What could be more exotic than that?

Well, let me tell you.

I've recently made a startling discovery: there's actually an entire country above us. With people and roads and everything. Being even further north than us, their weather is even more intolerable than ours. Talk about exotic.

This magical foreign land is called Canada.

For the first time in my life, I am international; having now taken several trips to this land of enchantment and wonder to our north. I know that most of my readers lack the foolhardy, thrill-seeking adventurous spirit that I possess; so you've probably never been to this mysterious soil to our north. What's up there, you wonder?

Wonder no more. I'll tell you all about it.

Canadians have a reputation of being friendly—and you see evidence of that right away. No sooner are you at the border than a nice Canadian appears to greet you and ask you all sorts of friendly questions: Where are you from, where are you going, what are you going to do when you get there?

As you drive into Canada, it looks almost normal. It seems like the real world until you look a little closer. For one thing, they use the metric system in Canada, so it's impossible to know if you're driving the right speed or how many liters (or kilowatts or whatever) of gas it will take to fill up your tank.

On the plus side, I'm fairly sure that you weigh less in metric—just like when astronauts walked on the surface of the moon.

There is at least one city in Canada. It is called Estevan. There may be more, but no one knows.

There are so many things to do in Canada! You can eat at McDonald's, or you can eat at a Chinese place, or you can eat at KFC, or you can eat at this sit down restaurant that I don't remember the name of. The possibilities are almost endless, and I've done them all.

But before you get too excited, let me warn you: it isn't a real McDonald's; it's a Canadian McDonald's. Again everything's just a little off. There's no Dr. Pepper at the pop machine, the barbecue sauce packet has both English and foreign-y words on it, and when you pay for your food they give you plastic Monopoly money as change.

The people are also polite. A little too polite, if you ask me. Imagine yourself at the KFC. A gentleman there is happy to let you order ahead of him when you inadvertently cut in front of him and his girlfriend in line. All of this niceness is very creepy. These people are obviously up to something; and you'd better figure out what it is before it's too late.

You take a seat in the booth at the KFC, looking over your shoulder to see what dastardly deed these Canucks are cooking up for you. You work yourself into a panic. You miss the good ol' U. S. of A. You long for your homeland—where the gas comes by the gallon and there are 60 minutes in an hour.

Then your food comes. And you see that they've given you gravy with your french fries. You hesitantly give it a taste. You realize that this fry and gravy combination is the greatest thing to ever happen in the history of humankind.

With cheeks stuffed full of gravy-soaked fries, you burst into a rousing chorus of "O! Canada." Tears stream down your face. You are home.

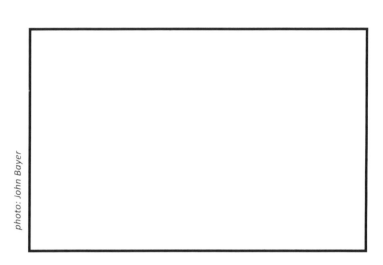

photo: John Bayer

I scoured through thousands of photographs looking for just the perfect picture of Canada. Here's what I found.

It is a beautiful land, ay!

IT'S NEVER TOO LATE TO RESOLVE TO BECOME A BETTER PERSON

O! Pioneer column originally published 3/27/13

We've reached the end of March, which can only mean one thing: Time to make a list of New Year's Resolutions for 2013. I'm told that other people create their lists of resolutions at the actual beginning of the new year. That's ridiculous. What a bunch of overachievers.

This leads naturally to my first resolution.

Stop procrastinating. A wise man once said, "Why put off until tomorrow what you can do today." I don't know who said it exactly. I've been meaning to look it up; but I just haven't gotten around to it yet.

Be more adventurous. I came to North Dakota for adventure. That's why I named this column "O! Pioneer." I moved to this small, rural community with the idea that I would jump into life here with gusto. I haven't been as successful as I had hoped.

I missed the fall hunting season. I didn't get to try my hand at ice fishing. In a column back in November, I pleaded that there be a curling season; and then when there was one, I failed to make it to a single game.

The problem is I am essentially a homebody. At the end of the day, I'd rather go home and curl up with a good book than go flying with someone in their two-seater airplane. (And by "good book" I mean "large bag of peanut butter M&Ms.")

131

But I haven't given up on the goal of being more adventurous. I think the key to reaching this goal in the coming year is to redefine the word "adventure." Sure, watching a rancher deliver calves is an adventure. But who's to say that it's any more daring than—I don't know—eating scrambled eggs that are slightly more runny than you're used to.

Get in shape. I've gained a solid 15 pounds since moving to North Dakota. This wouldn't be terrible, except that I was already a good 40 or 50 pounds overweight when I got here.

Every year, I resolve to "lose weight." And at the end of each year, when I look back over my list of resolutions, I'm disappointed that I failed to lose weight. That's why this year, I resolve to "get in shape." That way, at the end of the year (or next March or May) when I review my list; I can look at myself proudly in the mirror and say "Well, round is a shape." Then I can mark it off the list forever.

Don't smoke. I don't smoke. Never have. Don't plan to.

Still, I always include this on my resolutions list. It's nice to know that there is at least one item on my list that I will actually achieve.

Become a millionaire. I've never included this on a resolution list before, but it seems like a no-brainer. Who wouldn't want to be rich?

I'm just left with the small matter of how to make my fortune. If I had arrived in North Dakota a decade ago, I could have just bought up a bunch of land with mineral rights. Today those rights would be worth a fortune. But I suppose that ship has sailed already.

Unless, I could figure out how to build a time machine. Then I could go back in time and buy up all that cheap real estate. Or, I could just sell the time machine. Either way, I've stumbled upon a gold mine here.

Write more. I don't really have any intention of doing this, especially now that I'm rich. But since I tell everyone that I'm a writer, it would probably be a good idea to write once in a while. Or at least resolve to do so.

There you have it, my resolutions for 2013. In my next column, I will give you my list of resolutions for 2014. I want to get a jump on it—fight against procrastination. So be looking for that in the coming month. Next February at the latest.

AT THE MOVIES
PART I
from notes dated 4/6/13

These are historic times for the little movie houses across the nation. Everything is going digital. Awhile back, a group of people got together somewhere (probably Los Angeles) and decided that it was time for movies to go hi-tech. Since that time, the large theatre chains and indeed most every theatre in medium-sized and larger cities have gone digital.

But then there are the small theatres—the ones in small towns and rural areas throughout the nation. Most of them have remained in the past. They utilize 35 mm film projectors, where the trailers that run before the movie have to be physically cut and taped together onto the roll of film then threaded through the projector and focused manually by the projectionist. It's not a no-brain process; it requires someone who knows what they're doing. But it's also beautiful and romantic—it feels like old Hollywood. These small town theatres are keepers of the past.

The problem is, the movie studios don't want to be in the film business any more. Since the "important" places are all digital, having to create prints of their movies onto film seems archaic and just a plain waste of time. Each year, fewer and fewer prints are created. Small theatres have to scramble each week to find an available print (usually a copy that ran in another city the previous weekend) that they can get in time for Friday night's show.

I believe there is already one studio that has ceased making film prints entirely. Other studios will follow suit. Soon film prints will cease to exist —and with them a lot of small town theatres.

Single screen, weekend only, small town theatres are faced with a choice: convert your operation to digital or suffer a slow agonizing death. It seems like a fairly easy decision to make. But when you consider that the digital switchover runs in the neighborhood of $50,000, it becomes less clear. Many of these theatres show one movie three times over a weekend— they're hardly raking in the dough.

I don't really know how the rest of the country is faring, but in North Dakota it seems that most of the theatres have decided not to go gentle into that good night. Every regional weekly newspaper in these parts has had some article about their hometown theatre making the switch to digital. It was in Tioga's paper. Rugby's too. Kenmare. Stanley.

When I arrived in North Dakota, Crosby's Dakota Theatre was actively raising money for a digital movie projector. It had been going on for some time, I think. Money was coming in, but it takes a long time to raise $50,000 by putting out a donation box and selling old movie posters for $20 bucks a pop.

Then, in September, *The Journal* ran an article about the hows and whys of the Dakota Theatre going digital. The gist of the article was to this point—if we don't raise the remaining $40,000 soon, Crosby won't have a movie theatre much longer. The day after the newspaper came out, the theatre received a check for $10,000. The day after that, another check for $10,000 arrived. One check was from an area business, the other one was from a couple in the community.

A bunch of other checks of varying denominations came in during the next week or two. The people of Crosby had spoken: the Dakota Theatre would like a long and happy life.

I wish these movie studios would take a moment to look at Crosby and towns like it. If they knew the sacrifices made to keep the theatre open, maybe they wouldn't be so quick to write us off as nothing markets.

Fast forward to March, when the old projector and all its paraphernalia is removed and the new digital projector, computer and all the rest is put in its place. In some towns, the old projector would have been placed in a museum but here it's just thrown in a scrap heap. No point getting sentimental about it.

The new projector is amazing. The picture quality is terrific. The sound is better too. I can start and run this projector myself. Since there's no film to splice or to thread, no blurry picture to focus, no changing of lenses, any idiot like me with half a brain can get the thing going with just a push of a few buttons. Crosby has entered the digital age.

Attendance seems to be up these days. That may be because the picture and sound quality have improved. It might be because more oil people are in the area and need something to do during their downtime. It might be that the Dakota Theatre is showing movies closer to their opening date – since there isn't the mad scramble to find film prints from somewhere, anywhere. We've actually been able to show a few movies on their opening weekends. Maybe attendance is up for all of these reasons.

I love the Dakota Theatre and always will. But the romantic in me is saddened by the switch. Film is what started it all. It was the only game in town for decades. Before the advent of television, the movie theatre was one of the few connections a rural community had to the outside world. Sitting in that darkened room with a single beam of light spread across the wall. An image is conveyed on that beam of light. The image begins to move. You hear the flicker of the shutter as it moves in and out between frames. Occasionally you'd see a flare on the screen where the film had been damaged. Or a curly black line would dance across the screen as an errant hair worked itself out of the lens. These things reminded you that all of this was an illusion. But at the same time, it made it more real. Places you have never been and worlds you have never imagined suddenly came to vivid life before your eyes.

The digital age has brought us so much, but we've lost a few things along the way as well.

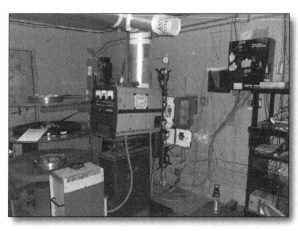

photos: Jonell Bayer

Above: The Dakota Theatre's former film projector. Note the large reel of film on the far left and the high-tech 'popcorn bucket ventilation system' at the top. It was old, but I loved it.

Below: The Dakota's current digital projector. I love this projector as well.

NORTH DAKOTA HAS A MELTDOWN AND SO DO I

O! *Pioneer* column originally published 4/17/13

It's the middle of April and spring has sprung in North Dakota. Well, maybe "sprung" isn't the right verb. It's the middle of April and spring has crawled into the room on its hands and knees gasping for air, bruised and bleeding like a drunk from a bar fight.

I'm reluctant to declare it spring because every time I start to get excited that temperatures are on their way up, another snowstorm comes through. In fact, it's snowing outside my window as I type these words. It's like North Dakota can sense my joy and says "not so fast, California boy."

But I'm at my wit's end (you may have noticed a lot less wit in my column lately), so I am just going to declare it to be spring. For me, winter began in late October after our first significant snowfall and I can't bear the thought of winter entering a seventh month. So I have decreed that it be spring.

A few days ago, I heard and then saw a small group of geese fly above me. So, if no one else does, at least five geese agree with me that winter is over. Although, now that I think about it, they did look like they might have been lost.

To be totally honest, I've been a little worried about the coming spring. As much as I would like to see winter go, I couldn't help wondering what my column would be about once I can no longer complain about the weather.

I needn't have worried. Spring in North Dakota is terrible, too.

When I moved here I was somewhat prepared for the piles and piles of this cold white stuff that would cover every surface of the earth. I say "somewhat prepared" because until you've actually experienced half a year straight of it, you can't be completely prepared.

People warned me about the winter. I was cautioned about this thing called "snow." But no one told me that when the mercury on the thermometer inches up, this white stuff turns into water! Lots and lots of water. (I know, I'm as surprised as you are!)

Another interesting fact is that when it gets cold again, this water doesn't turn back into snow. It turns into ice. Every street and sidewalk is magically transformed into an ice skating rink. To my amazement, I haven't fallen on my butt yet. However I have done a couple of accidental triple toe loops.

The other interesting thing about water is that when you combine it with dirt, it turns into mud. And it turns out that there is a massive amount of dirt in North Dakota. Ergo, there is now a massive amount of mud in North Dakota. ("Ergo" is a Latin word which means "Uff da.")

I hate mud; which is a shame, since mud loves me. It follows me everywhere I go. It's always there for me.

When I enter a room, I invariably leave a trail of mud in my wake. Most of the time, I don't even remember having stepped in mud. Sometimes, I haven't even come from outdoors.

On the bright side, because the warm up has been so slow, the meltdown of snow has also been slow. This has avoided a lot of potential flooding.

Of course, if you read this column on a regular basis, you know that I prefer not to look on the bright side.

A lot of disasters have been avoided this spring, but not all. From what I can tell every disaster that has occurred this spring has been localized to our office at work.

It started several weeks ago when black water started to drip from our ceiling. There is apparently a leak in our roof that the melting snow is working its way through. Of course, we have to wait until the snow melts completely before we can get up there to fix it. And by "we" I mean, whoever we hire.

After that, we noticed a structural problem around the back door. I didn't so much notice the structural problem as I noticed our own little swampland developing in the office. Water came pouring in from underneath the door. We scrambled to move what we could from the lake's path. The carpet became a marsh. The air grew musty. A little boy in the corner played the theme song from *Deliverance* on his banjo.

After some clean up, that problem seems to be behind us now. Just in time for the boxelder bugs to return. I haven't seen them anywhere else, just our office. The epicenter of Spring's wrath.

Now if I remember my Sunday School teaching correctly, this will soon be followed by frogs and then a swarm of locusts. Thankfully, I don't have a first born son or I'd really be scared. Ergo!

photo: Jonell Bayer

Years before I moved to the area, this building was Crosby's bowling alley. I love bowling and would have loved to have been able to!

Today, this building is 'the building that used to be Crosby's bowling alley.'

I WRITE A NEWSPAPER COLUMN, THEREFORE I AM

O! *Pioneer* column originally published 5/1/13

In a little over a week, I'll be making my first trip to Los Angeles since moving away. It's a weekend trip to see two friends get married. It's a short trip, but I'm glad for the chance to see some people and visit my old stomping grounds. Mostly, I'm looking forward to the fact that this time when I'm in Los Angeles, I will exist.

Let me explain that:

The most fundamental question of existence is "Who are you?" In Arizona, where I grew up, it was treated as a fairly straightforward question. Giving your name was considered a sufficient answer. In Los Angeles, however, the question "Who are you?" means "What have you done? Why would I know you?" You don't really exist there unless you have obtained some level of success that someone else could be jealous of.

When I left Los Angeles I was nobody—alone, fat, poor (I couldn't even afford a car) and without any accomplishments to speak of. I go back to Los Angeles a changed man—alone, fatter and not-as-poor (though I still can't afford a car). But now I have an accomplishment. I am an award-winning columnist.

Last week was great for my ego. It began with my first ever fan phone call. I've received many kind words about my column from people out and about. I've even gotten some emails and a few hand-written notes. But this was my first phone call. Her name was Linda. At least I think it was. I'm not really sure, because for five minutes we mostly spoke about me—my preferred subject of conversation.

Then this weekend at the North Dakota Newspaper Association annual convention, *O! Pioneer* received an award for best humor column. It was another boost to the ego. If I still lived in Los Angeles, I would finally have an answer to the question "Who are you?"

But I don't. I live in North Dakota, and here accomplishments like mine—that don't serve to better the community or put food on the table—don't hold the same weight. It's just ego. And here, "ego" is a four-letter word; like "vegetarian" or "Democrat."

About a month ago, I was in a social situation and a stranger came up to me and said, "I don't know you. Who are you?" The question was dripping with suspicion. I answered "John Bayer."

She shook her head and asked again: "Who are you?"

Thinking she hadn't heard me, I repeated "John Bayer."

If I had been holding a knife, it would not have been sharp enough to cut through the awkward silence that passed between us. I could tell from this lady's face that to her I did not exist.

I was scratching my head as I retold this story to a friend of mine. He grew up around here and knows the lay of the land. His name is Ryan. (At least I think it is. I'm not really sure; we mostly talk about me.)

He informed me that when you're asked "Who are you?" you are supposed to identify your lineage. The correct answer for me would have been: "I am John and Lois Bayer's boy." Not that this woman would know who they are either.

In small town North Dakota, heritage defines a person more than anything else. Are your people farmers or city folk? Are they Norwegians or Belgian?

Heritage is even important for your animals. At work, I have put together horse and bull sale catalogs for local sellers. Each animal listed in these books is described in depth. A family tree going back three generations is provided for each animal.

I marvel that not only can the sellers trace some dumb animal's lineage that far back, but that all of this information actually means something to potential buyers. For heaven's sake, the dumb animal writing this column can't even trace his family roots back as far as a horse!

Other than some Romanian on my father's side, I don't know where my people are from. We're not Norwegian, I don't think. And honestly, I couldn't even find Belgia on a map!

Oh well. For now, I'll live my life as a nobody in North Dakota.

Being part of the small town community. Enjoying the warmer temperatures. Writing my little (award-winning) column. Saving to buy a car again someday. Taking weekend trips to visit friends in California.

By the way, is anyone headed to Minot next Thursday evening? I need a ride to the airport.

photo: Jonell Bayer

Photographic proof that I am an award-winning writer. This should silence my critics once and for all.

And by 'critics' I mean 'family.'

WHAT THE FRACK?
(A FEW THOUGHTS ABOUT OIL)
from notes dated 5/9/13

Up until a few years ago, if you asked the average American, "What can you tell me about North Dakota?" their answer would have been: "Is Mount Rushmore in North or South Dakota?"

Today, the answer would be "isn't that where they found all that oil?" (Apparently, the average American likes to answer a question with another question.)

Yes indeed, the recent oil boom has garnered a lot of attention for North Dakota. Workers are coming here in droves to the only state in the union with more jobs than people. Environmentalists are decrying the dangers of "fracking" and would be happy if the whole operation were shut down completely. Suddenly, people are excited about North Dakota.

And I am, quite frankly, bored to tears.

I write about North Dakota, and these days anyone who writes about North Dakota has to write about oil. So I will do my duty. Ten, twenty years ago, you didn't have this problem. Then, you could write an entire book about North Dakota, entitled *No, Mount Rushmore Isn't Here*. And you'd open up to read. "No. We didn't move it. It was never here. Try the lesser Dakota down below."

Books were shorter back then.

The oil production in North Dakota just isn't of much interest to me. I didn't move here to work in the oil field. I didn't leave my wife and three young daughters behind in Bessemer, Alabama, and move to North Dakota with a hope and a prayer of finding work in order to support my beautiful girls. I didn't have to struggle to find a place to live, finally having to resort to living in an RV and dreading the harsh winter that was fast approaching.

That isn't my story. Although now that I read it back, I kind of wish it was. Man, if that guy wrote a book, I would definitely buy it.

My story is simple. I moved to North Dakota mainly to see what it's like to live in a small town. I'd always had romantic ideas about what life in Small Town, U.S.A. was like and I wanted to experience it firsthand.

If you're looking for the quintessential small town, you can't do better than Crosby, North Dakota. It's small—only about 1,100 people—but it's still the largest city in the area. You have to drive an hour to find a larger city. Thirty minutes if you count Canada. . . . you *never* count Canada.

Crosby is a modern place—I mean there are ATMs and cell phones and all that—but it feels like a Norman Rockwell painting. Main Street leading up to the county courthouse seems like a set they built to make a movie about a small town. It is too perfect.

There are plenty of small towns in North Dakota. Most of these towns were in steady decline before the oil boom hit. Many, even if there has been an upsurge in population, still look like no one lives there. It's like those homes where the owners have defaulted on their mortgage, so they decide for some reason to ransack the place on their way out. It's like that on a town-wide scale.

Crosby is different. Even during the declining years (before my time), the people of Crosby worked to maintain the town's beauty and fought to keep and even grow the local economy. The lifelong residents take pride in their city and it shows.

Crosby is on the upper edges of the Bakken Formation, where all this oil nonsense is happening. (Bakken is a Norwegian word which means "guy whose last name is Bakken.") Because of its position, the town has been affected by the oil industry, but not completely transformed by it like Williston and Watford City, and other towns. I'm grateful for this. I have a deep affection for Crosby—the town, the people, and the spirit—and I would hate to ever see that change.

At this point you're probably saying, "There sure hasn't been much talk about the oil industry in this essay about the oil industry."

My response is: "Hey buddy, who's writing this essay?"

To which you say: "Your guess is as good as mine."

The oil in this area is removed by a process called "fracking." I have no earthly idea what fracking is or how oil was accessed before this fracking method was developed or whether that was more or less dangerous than the current process. I know very little about how these things work.

I feel like there must be an easier way to access oil, though. I remember seeing a documentary once where a gentleman was able to get an oil well started on his own property simply by firing a shotgun into the ground. On further reflection, that was not a documentary but rather the opening title sequence to *The Beverly Hillbillies.*

Although I know nothing about fracking, I've heard of a lot environmentally- and ecologically-minded people speak out against it. It pollutes the air. It stresses out prairie dogs, keeping them up at night. It causes an old Lakota Sioux man to shed a single tear.

In the interest of full disclosure, I don't really trust most activists. Activists have taken it upon themselves to be society's overbearing mother. They don't think we should eat meat. They don't want us to buy normal light bulbs, even though the new bulbs give off less light and cause migraines. They don't want me to put my empty soda can in the garbage because that will cause the earth to get warmer somehow. Well, guess what activists? I already have an overbearing mother. She lives in Arizona. (Hi Mom!)

Also, you try living in North Dakota for awhile and then tell me that you wouldn't give a million dollars for a little global warming.

My biggest problem with all of these boys who cried 'oil' is that most of them have never set foot inside North Dakota. They say, "Fracking is destroying the land and the water and the air." And I look around the state and say, "It is?" Granted, I can't see the long term effects looking out my living room window. Then again, neither can the activists.

Now far be it from me to defend the oil industry—unless they want to pay me a truckload of money to do so—but I can see good and bad here.

First, the good. For one thing, it's been pretty good for the economy. There are lots of people working now that haven't been working for some time. In the last five years, while the rest of the nation was struggling through the recession, North Dakota was booming. Jobs are plentiful—not only in the oil industry but in every business in the western half of the state. A flood of new people have poured into a state that previously was seeing its numbers steadily decline. Unemployment is now about 3 percent—the lowest in the nation.

Also, there is at least one positive environmental impact. Water. When I first moved to Crosby, the water was yellow. Not yellowish. Yellow. This wasn't some terrible consequence of careless Big Oil. This is the way the water had been in Crosby for decades, as far back as people could remember. During my first month in Crosby, I was constantly flushing my toilet, thinking, "Why won't this pee go down?" After five or six flushes there would be the moment of realization, "That's right, it's not pee, it's the water that I drink." According to those in the know, the water was safe to drink, but I avoided that whenever possible. It not only looked yellow, it tasted yellow.

A little more than halfway through my time in Crosby, the city began getting its water from a different source. A pipeline was put in, sending us water from Stanley or Ray or some other place south of us. I don't remember. But I remember the first time I turned on my kitchen faucet and the new water came out. It wasn't yellow; it was invisible. Clear, like I'd vaguely remembered water being in my previous life.

That project, that pipeline, that water, was possible because there was now enough money around to fund a project like that.

I have plenty of bad things to say about oil too. Fracking does have a huge environmental impact – one that has nothing to do with trees and birds and the air we breathe. The feel of North Dakota—at least the western half of the state—is changing. It had already begun before I arrived, but I've been able to see its growth and development since I arrived.

The area doesn't have the infrastructure to support all of the activity that is currently taking place. Little two-lane highways are being torn to shreds by a deluge of semi and work truck traffic. There's no place to house all of the people here, and more people are arriving every day. New man camps and apartment complexes and extended stay hotels pop up seemingly overnight—stealing away more and more of the prairie landscape.

There's also a growing disparity between the haves and have-nots. The price of housing has probably tripled or quadrupled in the last six years. That's fine if you're an oil company buying up any apartments you can for your workers. You've got deep pockets. But there are plenty of people who need to rent who work at the Hot Stuff or the Hardware Hank. These folks are making a decent wage but they're not making that much fracking money. You've also got a farmer who's cashing in nicely from leasing the mineral rights to his property, while on the next farm over, there's no lucky payday awaiting them. That's got to have some impact on how you feel about the neighbors.

Further, the average oil man hasn't "moved" to North Dakota. His family is back "home." He works for three weeks straight and then goes to visit them for a week before coming back to work another three week shift. Now I admire that these men and women are doing what they need to in order to care for themselves and their loved ones. At the same time this "just passing through" attitude leads to more crime, less community involvement, and less concern for the care and upkeep of the environment. Cities like Williston feel like a town without a sheriff in a Western movie from the 1950s—only with newer cars.

Again, it comes down to a sense of community and civic pride. It's the reason that I love Crosby and it's the thing I fear the most about the oil industry being in North Dakota. I would hate to see my adopted home lose those things that make it Crosby.

photo: Gary M. Joraanstad

Here's a different oil thingy.

THE ONE-TIME OUTSIDER OFFICIALLY BECOMES A LOCAL

O! Pioneer column originally published 5/15/13

As I have mentioned many times in this column, I moved to North Dakota from Los Angeles. I am not, however, from Los Angeles. I grew up in Arizona. In fact, nobody is actually from Los Angeles. In a city of 13 million, all but 17 people moved there from somewhere else.

But there is a rule—I think it might be a city ordinance—that if you're able to survive in LA for at least two years, you're allowed to call yourself a native. I lasted four years.

I've lived in Crosby for almost 10 months now. I'm not sure what my status is. I'm not a native. You don't need me for that; plenty of people who were born here still live here.

Is it too soon to start calling myself a "local" at least?

I'm not sure. I still have a lot to learn. For example, I recently met someone who was posting flyers for a Syttende Mai Celebration. I asked "How do you pronounce that?" She told me. I then asked, "What is it?"

She looked at me as if I had just pulled a live buffalo out of my nose. I have since learned that Syttende Mai or "May seventeenth" is some sort of Norwegian independence day where Norway threw off the shackles of the tyrannical Swedes.

With all due respect to this woman, how was I supposed to know that!?

Growing up in Arizona, we only learn about one Independence Day. And that's Cinco de Mayo, a day to celebrate Mexico's victory in battle over their French occupiers.

(Side note: The Swedes? The French? Really? These folks must have been a lot tougher in the 1800s. Also, have you noticed how all these independence days—May 5, May 17, July 4—happen in the summer? I guess no one wants to fight injustice while hockey season is in full swing. But I digress.)

I also think I talk about myself too much to be a local. In LA no one knows who you are, so you're constantly talking yourself up and selling yourself to others. That's not necessary here, where everyone knows everyone. While in the big city people talk about themselves, in a small town people just talk about everybody else.

The final nail in my "local" coffin is that I still hate that Crosby siren. Hate it. I don't need a screeching howler monkey outside my window telling me it's 10 at night. I have a clock. Thanks, anyway.

On the other hand, I survived a North Dakota winter. And it was long. And I didn't fall on the ice a single time. And I'm still here. So that one thing trumps everything else. I am now officially a local.

As a local now, my first suggestion to you other locals is that it's time we stop letting outsiders come into our community. I don't mean to overstate the case, but these non-locals are ruining everything.

Now that it's getting warmer, they are arriving in droves. There's too many of them. I've had to resort to shopping on Saturday morning to avoid crowds at the grocery store. (That's my beauty rest time, people!)

Furthermore, outsiders don't understand our ways. I work at the movie theater on weekends and on more than one occasion I've had an outsider ask "What movies are playing?"

Movies? Really? As in more than one movie? Does this look like a megaplex to you? Many towns this size can't even keep a one-screen movie house open. Sorry sir, we don't have an IMAX 3D showing of *Iron Man 3* right now. Try Bowbells.

(To their credit, though; outsiders are usually delighted that our ticket prices are half—at least—of what you would pay in a big city. On the other hand, I once had a local use the word "expensive" to describe her $7 balcony seat.)

The other day as I was walking down Main Street, a woman got out of her car and popped into the post office. On the way, she set her car alarm.

Outsider!

Did she really think her car was going to be stolen in the 30 seconds it takes to check one's mail? I should give her the benefit of the doubt. Maybe she was mailing a package. That could take as many as two minutes.

Heck, I know locals who not only don't lock their car doors, they never bother to take the keys out of the ignition.

It's rubbing off on me. I myself now rarely lock the front door when I leave my house. And I was raised in a home where we always locked the door. Always. Even when we were home!

Despite my diatribe, I'm not too upset. These outsiders may be bothersome, but as a local I know to be patient. Come October, they'll all fly south for the winter with the geese.

Pictures of farm equipment.

Although I know less than nothing about farming, I include these photos because I am a firm believer in the philosophy "give the people what they want."

photos: Gary M. Joraanstad

BEING A CELEBRITY SHOULD COME WITH A FEW PERKS

O! Pioneer column originally published 5/29/13

My former home, Los Angeles, is the epicenter of Celebrity with a capital "C." There are famous people everywhere. I was in a coffee shop once when Tim Allen walked in. Another time, I stood a few feet away from Jennifer Love Hewitt. That was also in a coffee shop. I once watched entertainment reporter Billy Bush illegally park his car on the street. He then ran into a coffee shop. (Maybe Los Angeles isn't the land of Celebrity as much as is it the land of Coffee shops.)

Beyond actual famous people though, there is the allure of celebrity. Every day a new batch of young, bright-eyed wannabees get off the bus in LA with dreams of taking the town by storm and becoming a celebrity. What they don't understand is that the bus going in the opposite direction is filled with older, bleary-eyed never-weres who had just enough money to afford the ride back to their parents in Duluth.

It's not easy to become a celebrity in Los Angeles.

What these LA dreamers don't realize—and what I have learned—is that if you want to become famous, you don't move to southern California. You move to western North Dakota.

In all modesty, I feel safe in writing that I am a celebrity here. (Well, maybe not "all" modesty.)

Celebrity comes with perks. Strangers stop me on the street and ask, "Aren't you the guy. . .?" I've gotten fan letters mailed to me. Here is one particularly moving example: "Enclosed is a check for my newspaper subscription. By the way, I like the articles that one guy writes."

Still, it's not all gravy. Being famous in North Dakota isn't the same as being famous in Los Angeles.

For one thing, people don't kiss up to you here. Take my coworkers. They enjoy having fun at my expense. The other day, one of them asked me: "John, have you ever had Croom Caca?"

With a sour face I reply, "No, but I had German measles when I was two."

After the laughter dies down, it is explained to me that "Krumkake" is not a highly-infectious disease. Despite its gross sounding name, krumkake is actually some sort of Norwegian treat, that—based on the pictures I saw on the Internet—looks a bit like a waffle cone.

My coworkers are disappointed that I have never had krumkake. "Have you at least eaten sandbakkels?"

"No."

My coworkers shake their heads in dismay.

So, here is my dirty confession. Despite my severe sweet tooth, I haven't had most of your exotic treats. I've never had julekake or roommegrot or even oompa-loompas. There I said it. (For the record, I have eaten lefse on three separate occasions, so please don't run me out of town.)

But why should I? It's not like I moved to North Dakota and somehow suddenly knew the recipes for krumkake, roommegrot and uffda pie. The only reason I've had lefse is because it was cooked for me.

And that's when it hit me: celebrities in Los Angeles get free stuff all the time. So should I. Every time I come into work, there should be a plate of krumkake waiting for me. Friends should be handing me sandbakkels with a note that reads "Thinking of you." Strangers should be arriving at my door with dishes of lutefisk. (OK, I can live without that last one.)

As I think about it further, I actually have gotten some free stuff. One lady graciously mended my jeans after I had put a hole in them. Another person gave me the use of his truck several weeks ago when I needed to drive to Minot. He's still letting me use the truck today. And I have gotten quite a few free meals in my time here. (I've yet to pay for lefse.)

I suspect that I've gotten all of these freebies not because I'm a celebrity, though. The people in question are just generous by nature.

It's as if the celebrity treatment isn't just reserved for famous people like me. Oh well, I guess that I can learn to live with that.

Now if we could just get a decent coffee shop around here. . .

photo: Jonell Bayer

I would be remiss if I didn't include a picture of my parents: John and Lois Bayer. Here are my folks when they came up from Arizona to visit the Threshing Bee. . . and me, perhaps.

I know it looks like my dad is bored in this picture, but he's actually studying another tractor that's out of the frame. Don't worry, he is having a good time; he always looks like that.

WHAT'S IN A NAME?
PART III
from notes dated 6/19/13

If you ever decide to move to North Dakota, I'll warn you now that for the first six months, 90% of your time will be consumed with people correcting you on the pronunciation of their last name. You will get chided and laughed at. Kindergarteners will shake their heads and say, "How can you not be able to say a simple name like 'Svangstustromstadsonstreich'?"

North Dakotans are overall a sensible and pragmatic people, but there is one simple truth that they refuse to acknowledge. Their names are hideous.

As is usually the case, the root of the problem is the Norwegians.

Norwegian is an unpleasant and cumbersome language, which is why only Norwegians ever bother to learn it. And even they don't really want to bother with it. The majority of the people who left Norway for the U.S. in the first place, didn't do so to escape religious persecution, or for the hope of prosperity, but because they wanted an easier language to speak. And they wanted to experience what tacos tasted like.

Those men and women are long gone now, but they have left us the legacy of some truly strange names. So good riddance!

Now it would be impossible for one human to sort through all the eccentricities of these names. It would require a team of linguistic experts working around the clock, willing to sacrifice friendships and time with their families to understand it all. We would lose a few men, I'm sure.

Since I don't want anyone's death on my conscience, I'll settle for giving you a few quick tips for navigating through the maze of Norwegian names.

All of the surnames mentioned below are listed in the current Divide County telephone directory.

Tip #1: You always pronounce the 'K'

There are many names floating around these parts with a "Kn": Knudsen, Knutson, Knudsvig. You're going to be seeing this name written down and every word you've ever learned that started with "kn" is going to come flooding to your mind – knife, knowledge, knees, knave. You're going to open your mouth. Don't say it. Please, for the love of God, don't say, "You must be Thor Nootson."

You said it, ignoring my advice. You are now labeled as that weirdo who couldn't say "K-nutson." Out of towner! Don't worry, though, people around here will forget all about it in forty or fifty years.

Tip #2: Don't be afraid to put letters together in strange combinations

The letters "dsv" appear together in that order nowhere in nature, but as you've already seen, they exist in the surname "Knudsvig." Generally speaking, the Norwegians feel that vowels are overrated and love to throw as many consonants together as possible between vowels. Here are some examples of this principle (just from the "T" section of the phone book): Throntveit – Thvedt – Thomte – Tangsrud. I've heard each of these names spoken repeatedly in public and yet, as I look at them, I'm still only 60% certain how to pronounce any of them.

The name "Haugenoe" is an example that occasionally, the pendulum swings the other way and a name is loaded with vowels and sparse on consonants.

Names that a non-Norwegian has a fifty-fifty shot of pronouncing right the first time are terribly rare.

Tip #3: The letter A—a vowel so nice, we listed it twice

Once upon a time, maybe, there was an old Norwegian man named Elmer Nygard. One day he decided to add another 'a' to his name, as he loved the letter 'a' and had always lamented that his name only contained the one. But Elmer found that wherever he placed the 'a' he ended up with a totally different name. He didn't want to go through whatever time he had left as Elamer Nygard or Elmer Naygard, or God forbid, Elmera Nygard. Then he realized that if he placed the 'a' next to the other 'a' it still looked sort of the same. Perhaps he could get people to pronounce it the same as well. And at the ripe old age of 91, Elmer Nygaard was born.

I don't know what 'gaard' means in Norwegian—you have an internet connection, you look it up—but it's a very popular ending for names.

Nygaard – Legaard – Melgaard – Oppegaard – Melgaard

Tip #4: Why mess with a good thing?

There are several common endings to surnames beside 'gaard.'

'Strom' is another. Bergstrom – Strom – Landstrom

'Stad' is another. Joraanstad – Kostad – Kulstad – Lundstad – Lystad – Shefstad

Sometimes a name is created from combining the ends of two other names. Stromstad

There are apparently not a whole lot of potential letter combinations allowed in the Norwegian language, so if someone else has a name you like, you steal it. Thus Lars Hedahl has as neighbors, Erik Ledahl on one side and the Lovdahl twins on the other.

Down the street you have Haug, Haugen, Haugenoe and let's not forget Haugland.

It was getting too confusing for Luella Bakken living across the street from Luella Bakke, so she moved next door to the Fagerbakkes who vacation every summer with the Fagerland and the Fosland families.

Jim Andersen is occasionally invited over to dinner with the Andersons. If it's a real party, then the Andrists and the Andricks will stop by as well. If Cindy Lund is there and gets a little tipsy, she might turn to a Gillund or a Lundstad and ask, "Who am I again?" And the other party-goers will rail with laughter.

Tip #5: If you don't know with whom you're conversing, it's probably a *something*-son.

In North Dakota it's considered a mortal sin not to remember someone's name. If it's someone you haven't met before, then not knowing his or her name is merely a venial sin.

If you aren't great with names, keep in mind that the "sons" are by far the most abundant people in the area. Usually, the name ends in the more traditional "son." Other names conclude with the more exotic "sen."

If you're ever at a dinner party—you won't be; North Dakotans don't throw dinner parties—and you've forgotten with whom you are speaking, chances are it's a "son." As you end your conversation with them, say something like, "It's so good to see you again, Mr. *sumbleble*SON. I have to go now." That "*sumbleble*" is achieved by placing your hand over your mouth while pretending to scratch your nose. If done correctly, there is a 93% chance of success.

As Lutheranism teaches us, the Son will save us from our sin.

Here are some of the local 'sons' (keep in mind, this is in a county or about 2,000 people total): Andersen – Anderson – Benson – Borreson – Christensen – Christenson – Christianson – Ellingson – Ellison – Enerson – Erickson – Evenson – Frederickson – Gilbertson – Gunderson – Gustafson – Halvorson – Hansen – Hanson – Ingwalson – Jacobson – Jensen – Johnson – Knudson – Knutson – Larsen – Larson – Mathson – Monson – Nelson – Nielsen – Olsen – Olson – Paulson – Pederson – Petersen – Peterson – Rollofson – Rynearson – Semingson – Sigvaldsen – Simonson – Sorenson – Stenson – Swanson – Swenson – Thompson – Torgerson – Torgeson – Vassen – Wilson

I had a roommate in college named Christiansen. In Divide County, there are Christensens, Christensons and Christiansons, but no Christiansens. Thank God! It's reassuring to know that I live in a place with some good taste and discernment.

SOMETIMES IT TAKES A VILLAGE TO WRITE A HUMOR COLUMN

O! Pioneer column originally published 6/12/13

I'm looking out my living room window as I write today. The birds are singing. The flowers are blooming. The temperature outside is lovely. Springtime has definitely arrived in all of her glory.

How depressing!

Over the 10 months that I have been writing this column, *O! Pioneer* has quickly evolved into *O! John Finds Something Else to Complain About.* And for once, the weather in North Dakota is not cooperating with me.

If I were a farmer I would complain about all the rain that we've had lately. But since I'm not, as long as the rain stays outside where it belongs I'm content.

(I don't know much about agriculture. The one thing I've learned about farming since moving to North Dakota: no matter what the weather conditions, a farmer gets to complain about them. It's too cold. It's too hot. It's too wet. It's too dry. It's too temperate. . . . I wonder if God meant for me to be a farmer.)

Since I don't have anything to complain about, I've decided to write about all the things that people have asked me to write about over the last year. When you're a writer, people always try to give you advice on how to do it better. "I enjoy your writing. But why don't you write about. . ."

I don't think this happens so much in other professions. I don't go down to where you work and say, "That field would look so much nicer if you planted the wheat in zigzags instead of straight lines." (Maybe I wasn't meant to be a farmer.)

To date, no columns have been born out of these suggestions. That's because they're always terrible. But today I've decided to write about them. I figure a terrible column would be better than a huge blank space in the middle of the newspaper page.

The 'why don't yous' come in categories. In the first category we have things I know nothing about.

Why don't you write about man camps? Why don't you write about Hostfest? Why don't you write about Bismarck? Why don't you write about calving?

Alright, here goes. I've never been to a man camp. I've never been to Hostfest. I've been to Bismarck once for a workshop, but I spent the entire day in a hotel conference room. So in my experience: Bismarck has harsh florescent lighting and uncomfortable seats, but there is an ample supply of pop at the table in the back.

I've never assisted in the birthing of a calf but I think I'm safe in saying "It's gross and disgusting."

The other category of 'why don't yous' are the ones where people want me to chastise other people for them. So for the record: New arrivals need to make more of an effort to become a part of the community. The community in general doesn't attend events that support the arts. You should floss every day. (No one gave me that last one. It's just a good idea.)

Yesterday someone asked me "why don't you write a column about North Dakotans' obsession with ranch dressing?"

I was very bothered by this suggestion. More so than any other I've ever received. Why? Because it actually sounds like something I would complain about. And someone else thought of it first!

I don't eat ranch dressing very often, which may explain why the Great North Dakota Ranch Dressing Pandemic has gone unnoticed by me until now. But as I think back, I know it's true. All the dinners I've attended with multiple bottles of dressing on the table. All the requests at restaurants "could I have another two cups of ranch?" And nary a salad in sight.

Whenever I discover a problem of this magnitude, I always ask myself "is there a way for me to make a buck here?"

The answer is "yes." I have decided to open a restaurant. It's called 'The Ranch.'

Every menu item at The Ranch features a creative use of ranch dressing. Our burger features a sea of ranch dressing injected into the center of the patty before cooking. That comes with a side of Ranch Taters—shoestring potatoes deep fried in a vat of boiling ranch dressing. And don't forget dessert. The Pie a la Ranch cannot be beat. It's a slice of apple pie with a healthy scoop of ranch dressing ice cream on top. Of course, every menu item comes with a side of ranch dressing.

We're open every day for dinner and supper. Come on in and have a bite. Then feel free to tell me how much you love the restaurant and then tell me all the things I should be doing to make it better.

photo: Jonell Bayer

Like all major metropolises, Crosby, North Dakota has it's own airport.

Be sure to book your flights early.

YOU CAN LEAD A HORSE TO NORTH DAKOTA, BUT . . .

O! Pioneer column originally published 6/26/13

The Roman Empire fell about 1500 years ago, yet its influence remains. I know of at least three expressions from that time or about that time: Rome wasn't built in a day. All roads lead to Rome. When in Rome do as the Romans do.

That's the kind of staying power North Dakota should be after. This oil boom isn't going to last forever. We're going to need something to keep people coming here for generations to come. I think a campaign of catchy slogans like those Romans had will do the trick.

I've come up with a few to help get the ball rolling.

1) When in North Dakota, do stop your danged cell phone conversation and actually talk to the woman who's ringing up your groceries.

It's not as catchy as the "When in Rome" one, but it contains the sentiment I want to convey. This isn't Los Angeles. This isn't New York. This isn't even Florida (thank God). There's a different pace, a different style of doing things, a different elán. (Elán is a fancy French word that means Uff-da.)

I've seen a lot of people barrel in here like a bull in a china shop. Some don't seem happy here, and I think it's a problem of their own making. Life is a whole lot easier when you learn to take the pulse of your surroundings and adapt to it.

My second new North Dakota saying is based on the ancient Zen riddle: If a tree falls in the forest and there's no one there to hear it, did it make a sound? The North Dakota equivalent would be:

2) If an event happens in North Dakota and there was no guest book to sign, did it really take place?

In the little less than one year since I moved here, I have signed more guest books than in the other 36 years of my life combined. I've signed books in churches. I've signed books at dinners. I've signed books at seemingly abandoned historical landmarks. Heck, I've even manned at least two guest books myself—forcing others to legitimize an event by forcing them to sign a book that will never be looked at again. By anyone.

Next to the guest book is always the obligatory basket or jar for the "free will offering." Until I moved to North Dakota I had only seen that phrase used at church-sponsored events. But in North Dakota the phrase is used at any event that would require a guest book. So all of them.

In the church I grew up in, "free will offering" was a way of saying "This is costing us a lot of money to put together, but it's a God-thing so we feel weird asking you to pay up."

In North Dakota, however, it means something else entirely. "Free will offering" can be loosely translated as "Look, this thing is free. Ole donated the hamburgers. Lena and Hilda are donating their time to cook the meal. But you're Norwegians and wouldn't feel right eating for free, so here's a bucket to put your ten-spot in."

And you probably end up putting a 50 in there instead of a ten-spot. And Ole will pitch in a ten-spot even though he already bought all the food.

Because most North Dakotans I have met are generous with their money and their possessions. Sometimes generous to a fault.

I was at the movie theater a month or two ago. A woman was sitting in the lobby—her empty popcorn bucket on the table beside her—waiting for a fresh batch to be popped. Another woman came up to her with a rolled up bill in her hand and attempted to place it into the bucket. When called on this, she said "Oh, I thought you might be raising money for the high school or something."

You are a charitable people. There's an old expression that "Charity begins at home." But I have found that in North Dakota:

3) Charity begins at 7:30 p.m.

No deep meaning here. I've just noticed you all like to start things on the half hour. It's like every event planning meeting comes to: "Starting at seven will be too early for folks who have to travel in from other towns. But starting at eight will make for a late night for people who have to work in the morning. Let's split the difference."

North Dakotans believe: Why inconvenience one group of people, when it's just as easy to inconvenience everyone?

That's all I have so far. If you have any other new catchy phrases, come on by where I work. I'll have a book where you can write down your ideas and sign your name. And feel free to leave a little something in the jar next to the book.

photos: Gary M. Joraanstad

There are really only two seasons in North Dakota: Winter and Construction.

So, there is absolutely no good time of year to be on the roads.

REVENGE IS A DISH BEST SERVED HOT WITH ZERO HUMIDITY

O! Pioneer column originally published 7/10/13

This is it. This is my moment to shine. This is the column I've been waiting nine months to write.

Let me take you back: It was October. The mercury on the thermometer no longer rose above the 50s. So naturally, I started wearing my coat.

That's when the looks started. That's when people began to ask, while choking on their own disbelief, "Are you cold?"

That's when I made this vow: "Just wait until summer, when it's 80 degrees and you're complaining about the sweltering heat. I'll be loving every minute of it. That's when I'll get my revenge."

See, I was born and raised in southern Arizona. I'm conditioned to expect 80 degrees in March. By July, there have already been 30 days of temps over 100 degrees. It's the environment I thrive in. I've never liked the cold. I'm what we call in Tucson "a desert rat."

I arrived in North Dakota last July during the Divide County Threshing Show. Someone told me that it was the hottest weekend so far that year. I found that hard to believe since it was only in the 90s. I happily strolled the grounds that weekend, delighted for the relief from the temps in Los Angeles, where I had just come from. Meanwhile, everyone else walked around with buckets to scoop up their loved ones in case they melted.

A week or so later, I attended a church service. Everyone was quite apologetic that there was no working air conditioning and only two fans at the front of the church for cooling. I estimate that it was about 78 degrees in that building—warmer than I'm used to, but quite manageable. I found it to be an enjoyable service.

I don't think that was the case for the other worshipers. They looked pained and unfocused. Many were fanning themselves with the church bulletin. An elderly woman beside me burst into flames.

That first summer here was great for me. But like all good things it came to an end much too quickly. Summer gave way to autumn and then two weeks later, winter. Winter for me, anyway. You all were still wearing shorts and tank tops while I was zipping up my parka.

But through all the stares and teasing comments, I knew that summer would return. That's when I would get my revenge. As you pant like a dog on your way to the post office, I would just shake my head and say "You're not hot, are you?"

And of course, I'd write this scathing column that would make you feel ashamed for teasing me in the first place; and also for always picking me last for sports back in middle school. (That "last for sports" thing may not have been you. Sorry, I got a little carried away.)

Turns out that there is one little problem with my master plan of revenge. I can't believe I'm admitting this; but now that the temperature has started to climb into the 80s, I'm a little hot.

Spending just one year in North Dakota has turned me into a heat wimp. Our seven month winter has thickened up my blood just enough that I can't handle heat anymore. The desert rat is dead.

I'VE BECOME EVERYTHING I DESPISE!!!

I spend most of my time indoors. I don't really want to go anywhere because of the heat. I've become as much of a homebody during the summer as I was during the winter.

Also I'm tired. I can't get a good night's rest; not just because my bedroom is too warm but also because there's only five hours of darkness a night. When you grow up in a home that is closer to the equator than it is to the North Pole, a long day is when the sun sets after 7 p.m. I can't handle all this sun.

So, I've been robbed of my revenge. In the end it seems, the upper hand always goes to North Dakota. I guess I will be reduced to two weeks in the autumn and two weeks in the spring where I actually enjoy the weather. At least I'll never run out of things to complain about in this column. That's my promise to you, the reader.

photo: Jonell Bayer

Like other major metropolises, Crosby has its own public transportation system.

Rides are $1 per leg of your trip.

THINGS I WILL NEVER UNDERSTAND ABOUT THIS PLACE

from notes dated 7/17/13

I arrived in North Dakota one year ago today. I've learned so much in that time about the culture of rural Midwestern life. But I realize that there are just some things that I'll never understand.

Why is everyone so gung ho about rhubarb?

Rhubarb is the quintessential dessert vegetable in North Dakota. (I consider "dessert vegetable" an oxymoron to begin with—don't get me started on carrot cake—but that's a discussion for another time.) I've had rhubarb in pie. I've had it in a milkshake. And yes, I've had it in cake. Why is it in everything here? It has a strange color, a strange texture, a strange flavor. Sure, if you add enough sugar to whatever you're making, it's palatable. But if you have to disguise the flavor of something in order to eat it, just don't eat it. The leaves of the rhubarb plant are actually poisonous to human beings—do you think that might be God trying to tell us something? My mother tells me that when I was very young, I loved to eat raw rhubarb. Thankfully, I grew out of it. Unfortunately, North Dakota is still going through its 'rhubarb phase.'

Nobody walks.

In Los Angeles, since it's constantly congested with traffic, they say, "It's not a walking town." But it's not true. You might not be able to walk from one end to the other in a day, but people certainly walk around their own neighborhoods—for exercise, to take the dog out to do his business, and yes, even to get from point A to point B.

Crosby, on the other hand, is really not a walking town. This is strange since an able-bodied adult could literally walk from one end to the other in under an hour. A less able-bodied adult could probably still do it in two hours if she put those tennis balls on the legs of her walker. If you happen to be on the central strip of Main Street, you'll probably walk from business to business, but that's it. In LA, if you live within a mile of where you work you'd probably end up walking most days. In Crosby, if you walk to work, regardless of the distance, people assume your car is in the shop.

Before John F. lent me his truck, I walked everywhere—to work, the movie theatre, the grocery store, the drug store, and to the library. In all of those travels it's amazing the number of people I didn't meet.

A few people walk for exercise. They'll leave the house, walk around the city, or even out of town—up to the Crosby 'airport' or maybe even as far north as the country club. Then they'll head back home, get into their car and drive to the bank.

During the three months out of the year when it's not snowing, Crosby is idyllic—a Main Street that looks like it's from the 1950s and rows of charming houses. It's a real Norman Rockwell painting complete with birds singing and children playing. People should be out walking, enjoying it all. But people being people, most of the time we don't know how good we have it.

Auctions.

They have auctions around here all of the time. During the non-winter months, I doubt there's a week that goes by where you're not within a thirty minute drive of an auction. There are estate auctions, and moving sale auctions, and farm equipment auctions, and collectibles auctions, and gun auctions, and vehicle auctions, and even house auctions, and help-me-get-rid-of-all-this-stuff-I-got-at-auctions auctions.

At work, I design and print the advertising posters for some of these auctions. As they came in one after the other, I used to think, "I will never understand why North Dakotans are so into auctions."

Then I went to an auction. Now I think, "I will never understand why the rest of the world isn't into auctions the way we are."

Unless it's farm equipment or vehicles, the auctions are usually held indoors, in a large open space venue. I like to go to the one held at the old hockey rink because you know if they had to rent a space that large, there's going to be a lot of crap.

The key is to get there early. You want to have a chance to look around and scope out the best stuff. There are two phases to the auction. The second phase is the one we're all familiar with—everyone sitting down holding a number, the auctioneer's assistant holding up a pair of solid gold candlesticks, and the auctioneer in a vocal frenzy "I-have-75-here-who'll-give-me-80-75-who'll-give-me-80-80-here-will-anyone-give-me-90."

Before that happens, though, there is what I call "the box phase." This is the part of the auction that I love. In one section of the hockey rink are all of these cardboard boxes set on the floor. The boxes are open, so you can see what's in them. These are the items they have deemed unworthy of individual auctioning. So instead, the group of interested buyers follows the auctioneer around from box to box as he asks, "Anybody give me a buck for this one?" Sometimes, they will even group boxes together, if they aren't selling too well, or if the auctioneer is in a hurry to get to the big ticket items. My best score was a milk crate full of vinyl records plus two additional boxes for a dollar.

I love it. Because when you get home, the fun continues as you dig through and see what else is in the box. Maybe you bought the box for the old timey phone, but it also has a postcard from the 1910 World's Fair and old cans of motor oil, unopened.

But then, if you're like me, your enthusiasm starts to fade as you realize, there's a lot of junk in this box of junk. Halfway through, you decide that you'll sort it all out some other time. The box goes into the garage. Much later, you look in the garage and think, I need to get rid of all this junk. So you donate the box to another auction, where it is bought and the whole process starts over.

The circle of life.

How'd I get so fat?

The moment you step foot on North Dakota soil, you gain ten pounds. I say that to people and they laugh; but I'm not making a joke. Seriously, when I stepped off that plane in Minot, North Dakota, on July 17, 2012, I could feel it. Ten pounds. *Whoomp!* (or whatever sound ten pounds attaching itself to your body sounds like.)

Since then I've gained another twenty or thirty pounds—I'm afraid to look—which seems impossible since I'm nowhere near a McDonald's. I wonder if gravity is different here.

I can't tie both shoelaces in one stretch anymore. I have to stand up and catch my breath between shoes. My snow boots don't have laces. . . . I guess winter's not so bad.

North Dakotans fear spices.

Culturally speaking, it seems that the closer you are to the equator, the more heat and spice you like in your food. The food gets milder the farther away you get. I'm not sure why that is, but it seems true. North Dakota is about a million miles north of the equator. Norway, where many North

Dakotans trace their roots, is on the planet Saturn—approximately 1.2 billion kilometers from the earth's equator. (I don't know how far 1.2 billion kilometers is, since I'm an American, but I imagine it's at least a couple of days' drive.)

A good North Dakota spice rack contains salt, pepper, and some mysterious thing called chicken flavoring. Oregano, basil, cumin, and cayenne pepper are like witchcraft or the occult—something you shouldn't mess with or even joke about.

There's one Mexican restaurant in the county. The food is pretty good, but they do dial down the flavor for the North Dakota palate. One time while I was there with a group, a member of our party placed her order, then she reconsidered, asking, "Is that spicy?" The waitress assured her that it wasn't. Then came the follow up question, "But is it spicy for a Norwegian?"

I've asked it before and will ask it again: why, oh why, does that insufferable siren go off every day at noon and 10 p.m.?

photo: John Bayer

To make life safer for the three people in Crosby who walk, the town had a new sidewalk installed on the Farm to Market Road. One day, my friend Holly and I decided to take the sidewalk out for a spin. This picture is us at the end of the line.

The large obstruction at the bottom of the picture is my ample, North Dakota gut.

YOU CAN'T SPELL 'FASHION ICON' WITHOUT 'I'

O! Pioneer column originally published 7/24/13

One thing I like about living in North Dakota is that people don't care about how they look. Wait, that came out wrong. What I mean is that looking good isn't important to people in North Dakota. No, that's not any better.

What I mean to say is: everyone here looks awful.

Sorry. Sorry. Let me start this over.

My former home, Los Angeles has what you would call a fashion culture. Everyone is obsessed with not only how good they look, but with making sure they look and act like everyone is supposed to look and act this month. Los Angeles is a place where you get collagen injections and Brazilian waxes, eyebrow threading and coffee enemas. And I understand the women there get some weird things done, too.

North Dakota isn't so obsessed with fashion. I fit right in. I've been called a lot of things through the years—many of them I can't repeat—but "fashion conscious" has never been one of them.

So that should be the end of it. But I'm a kind of celebrity in these parts (as I've told you on many occasions). And one of the most important jobs a celebrity has is setting the latest fashion trends. I take my role as celebrity very seriously (as I've told you on many occasions); so I have decided to become a fashion icon.

My fashion tips are below. Incorporate them into your life and then you can be just like me (which, as I've told you on many occasions, is what you want to be.)

Fashion Tip #1: Make sure the clothes that you love the most are the largest clothes in your closet.

That way when you move to North Dakota and gain 30 pounds in a year and only have three shirts that still fit you, they will at least be the shirts you like the most.

Tip number one leads nicely into the next tip.

Fashion Tip #2: Don't freak out about your weight.

People say this all the time—even in LA—but they don't really mean it. Weight matters.

Even at my lowest weight in Los Angeles (a good forty pounds less than I am today), there was never an event I attended where I was not the fattest guy there. But nowadays when I go out. . . OK, I'm still the fattest guy, but I have to work a lot harder to retain my crown.

Fashion Tip #3: Work shoes go with everything.

Now some people claim that a brown work shoe doesn't pair well with a dress shirt and khaki pants. Or with your best Sunday suit. I say, "They do now."

Work shoes are the only ones I wear these days. I don't like wearing dressier shoes because they get covered with mud or dust so easily around here. And North Dakota has worn the soles of my sneakers down to practically nothing.

Sure the work shoes don't "match" or "go with" most of the clothes that I own; but fashions that coordinate are so last season. Welcome to the John Bayer era of fashion.

Fashion Tip #4: Random facial hair is the hottest new look.

I don't know why, but when I shave, I seem to be incapable of removing all of the hair on my face. While I'm shaving, everything looks fine. Two hours later, though I'll look in a mirror and notice an unshaven patch in the corner where my upper lip and nose meet. Or a square of stubble under my jawline. And there's always one random hair on my upper cheek - it's about 2 inches long but I never see it until I'm 30 miles away from the nearest razor.

I have two options here: One is to grow up and learn how to shave properly. The other option is to pretend that my mistake was intentional. I'll go with the latter.

So guys, it's time to start shaving haphazardly (or better yet, with your eyes closed) and start looking more fashionable. Like me.

And ladies. I don't want you to feel left out here. When it comes time to shave those legs, feel free to only shave the left one. It will not only put you on the "cutting" edge of fashion but it will "shave" a lot of wasted time from your morning routine.

For good measure, I have taken the additional step of growing extra hair out of my nose and ears. I know this happens to a lot of guys; but most men don't start doing this until they are in their 50s or 60s.

This just goes to show how truly fashion forward I am.

photo: Chrissy Running

The Dakota Theatre all lit up.

I love this place.

AT THE MOVIES
PART II
from notes dated 8/3/13

The city of Crosby, North Dakota isn't world famous, but it should be. Crosby's local movie house, the Dakota Theatre, claims to have the best popcorn in the world. And you know what? I think it does.

People come to the theatre every weekend just to buy popcorn—they don't even stay for the movie. When my parents and sister came to visit me last month, I bought some Dakota popcorn so that we could have a 'movie night' back at the Strawberry Palace.

A few days ago, my sister took my dad to the movies back in Arizona. On the phone, I asked him how the movie was. He said, "It was good. But their popcorn didn't compare with yours."

Why do I go on about popcorn? Well, I work for the Dakota now. I am contractually obligated to talk up the popcorn. We use real cream butter, not some processed you-don't-know-what-it-is ingredient.

The other stipulation on my contract is that when asked, I'm not allowed to say that a movie is bad. If I love a movie, I can say "I love this movie." If I hate a movie, I can say "I've heard it's really good."

I refer to the Dakota Theatre as just "the Dakota." It sounds cool. I'm the only one who does this. I don't understand that. We shorten everything else around here: a farmer goes to college to study *ag*, he gets a soda down at the *c-store*, and he checks into the hospital for his *tri by surg*. Why can't we shorten the name of the movie theatre? But we can't. But I'm going to anyway.

I started working at the Dakota back in January on Friday and Saturday nights. I love it. I've always wanted to work in a movie theatre. There's a magic about them. They connect us to other places, and to the past in ways that I find hard to articulate.

Our popcorn is available in small or large.

On the nights that I work, I try to be the first one there. That way I get to do it all—start the movie projector, get the popcorn going (available in plain, butter or cheese), get the box office set up. I love it.

I even like sweeping the theatre before the next show. Though I will say, I'm absolutely mortified by the number of grown adults who consider the floor of a movie theatre the same as a trash can. If you're not going to eat the rest of your popcorn (popped fresh each night) don't just dump it on the floor. You wouldn't toss your leftover fries on the floor at Denny's—maybe at Waffle House, but not Denny's – so don't do it here.

After the rest of the crew arrives and we finish the set-up, we take to our posts. I typically man the box office while the others handle concessions. I love working with the theatre crew. There are three managers—Ed and Chrissy and Andrea. And there are the teenagers—Brittany and A.J. and Zoe. Being neither a leader nor a girl in her teens, I'm an anomaly. But we all play a part in keeping this vital piece of community up and operational. I think that bonds us together.

Tickets are $5 for kids (3-12), $6 for adults and $7 for the balcony. These are insane prices. If memory serves me right, the cheapest ticket you can get in LA for a first run movie is now $8. And that's for an early show on a weekday. A ticket on Saturday night runs over $15 or $16. And concessions are going to run you double what they do here. The first time new people come into the theatre—usually oil people—they're shocked by the low prices of our tickets and our concessions.

A small plain popcorn is only $1.25.

We get new people in about every weekend. I like that. Many of them are just in town for work and aren't really a part of the community. The Dakota is one of the few points of connection between them and the town where they now live.

There's a lot you have to explain to a newcomer, though. The first thing they don't seem to understand is THIS IS NOT A MULTIPLEX. Newcomers like to ask what movies—plural—are playing this weekend. Sorry folks, we show one movie per weekend—Friday, Saturday and Sunday nights at 7:30—on our one solitary screen. The Dakota is a narrow building, so where do they think these other screens are hiding out? That's just a door to the bathroom, sir, not the wardrobe that takes you to Narnia.

You also have to explain to newcomers that we do things a little differently in a small town. For one thing, you can put that credit card away, we only take cash or check. There's an ATM at the bank across the street if you need money. No you don't get a ticket. I am both the ticket seller and the ticket taker, so I'll just hold onto it. There's really no point in me handing it to you and you handing it right back to me. Speaking of tickets, is that your car parked in front of the theatre? You'll have to move it, that's a fire zone. I know you don't see a red curb. The red paint faded away long before you were born, but the memory of it lives on, and you'll get ticketed. No, those are not the stairs to the balcony. There are no stairs to the balcony. The balcony is a set of comfy chairs set in the back of the theatre. Why do we call it the balcony? Because we've always called it the balcony. This is North Dakota—we believe it's better not to ask questions.

Yes, you can get extra cheese on your cheese popcorn for no additional cost.

Locals come with their own challenges. They won't tell you what they want, for one thing. A family will come in. The mom, presumably, will come up to my ticket window. And that's it. She might hand me money but she doesn't say anything. Now, this is the point at which you tell me how many tickets you're purchasing and how many are children and how many are adults. God chose to give me charm and dashing good looks, but He drew the line at psychic ability. I don't know what you are doing until you tell me what you are doing.

Do these folks do this at other places? At the restaurant, do they just stare into the waitress' eyes until she finally says, "I'll just bring you the special." Even if it's just a lone guy who comes in, he still has to tell me if it's a regular seat or a balcony. I get this silent treatment at least twice a night and I find the whole thing creepy and weird.

Also, everyone wants to pay with hundred dollars bills. I say, "one adult, that will be six dollars," and he hands me a picture of Benjamin Franklin. I only have $150 in my till to begin with. By the second Ben Franklin, I'm having to run in the back to make more change. It's not unusual to have to run back to the safe two or three times a night. Don't get me wrong, I love Ben. In fact, my wallet and I would like to see more of him. I'm just saying it's okay to break out an Alexander Hamilton once in a while.

(Incidentally, neither Benjamin Franklin nor Alexander Hamilton were ever president of the United States, but they've both made it onto our currency. So I guess there's still hope for me.)

Despite its quirks, I'd rather work at a movie theatre than, say, a dentist's office. The people at the theatre are there because they want to be; unlike the dentist's office, where people are there because they should really get this thing taken care of. At both places there are terrible, grating sounds— whether it's a whirring drill used to break through a tooth's enamel or a dramatic speech delivered by Dwayne "The Rock" Johnson. But in a week, The Rock will be gone and the drill will still be there.

At the dentist's office, popcorn eating is discouraged. Here at the Dakota, if you bring in your own tub, we'll fill it with buttered popcorn for $5.

THIS IS THE COLUMN WHERE I WRITE ABOUT WRITING A COLUMN

O! Pioneer column originally published 8/14/13

"What is your column about?"

I get asked this question a lot. Sometimes from people who didn't know that I write a column. Sometimes from regular readers curious about the subject of my next installment.

My answer: "What's my column about? . . . It's about 750 words."

Reading *O! Pioneer* is kind of like watching a television sitcom.

A sitcom starts with a thin premise. Lucy wants to be in show business but Ricky won't let her. Wilbur's horse Mr. Ed can talk. John Bayer complains about how great life in North Dakota is.

The premise isn't really important. It's just a means for getting to the jokes. Usually, there are only about three or four jokes that get repeated over and over again. Lucy and Ethel get into some jam trying to get Lucy into the limelight. Wilbur's friends think he's crazy as he goes to the barn and talks to himself. John Bayer complains about the weather and/or lovingly insults Norwegians.

It's good for a few laughs. In the case of a sitcom, it's over in 30 minutes just before you're in danger of becoming bored with the whole thing. In the case of *O! Pioneer*, it's all over in 750 words; about 150 words after you've already lost interest.

A day later, you remember the characters but probably not what the show was about. But it doesn't matter because Lucy's going to do almost the exact same thing next week. And so will Wilbur. With me, you usually have to wait two weeks; but that's probably enough time for you to fully recover.

In the final analysis *O! Pioneer*, like television sitcoms, isn't very important. I know that sounds like I'm insulting my own column but I'm not. I love my column.

I love that it's not important. I love that it's not about what's going on in the world. I don't debate the issues of the day, or try to sway public opinion (except my campaign to silence the daily bomb raid sirens). *O! Pioneer* is solely about making people laugh. Just like a sitcom.

I know about sitcoms. I grew up watching them, of course. But I also grew up thinking, "I could write that." Eventually, I could write that became I want to write that.

I went to film school to learn how to make sitcoms. After film school, I moved to Los Angeles with the dream of writing and producing television comedy.

After four years in Los Angeles, I was feeling burned out, and the dream took a sharp detour into North Dakota.

And here in North Dakota I've been given some wonderful gifts. Writing was becoming a chore for me, and in the last year I've started to enjoy it again. Seeing my words in print on a regular basis is such a treat as well. The greatest experience for me has been people coming up to me—which happens all the time—to tell me they laugh at *O! Pioneer*. These are gifts I am eternally grateful for.

Although my sitcom writing dream took this wonderful detour, ultimately the dream still lives. So it is with extremely mixed emotions that I need to let my readers know that I have made the decision to move back to Los Angeles. In a little over a month, I will be leaving North Dakota and heading back into the trenches of Hollywood trying once again to make my mark in television.

I have a couple more columns to write before I leave. My hope is that you all will stay with me to the bitter end. (Don't worry: the end won't be bitter at all. In fact, it may even have a couple of jokes in it, unlike this current column.) My other hope is that when I pass you on the street you won't shake your head at me and say "you're leaving?" in such a way that it sounds like I'm abandoning you personally. I'm not. Or maybe I am; but it's only because North Dakota has a terrible sitcom industry.

Moving back is scary; but I have a little more confidence knowing that I will be taking along all the gifts that you have given me.

And even though that last sentence would have been a great note to end on, I haven't quite made it to 750 words yet.

Can you believe this weather? Uff da!

There, that should do it.

photo: Gary M. Joraanstad

One of my biggest surprises in coming to Crosby was the discovery that there are seagulls in this very much landlocked state.

Very, very confused seagulls.

IF YOU'RE ANGRY AND YOU KNOW IT, CLAP YOUR HANDS

O! Pioneer column originally published 8/28/13

You're angry with me.

In my last column, I told you about my decision to move back to California next month. And now I get the distinct feeling that people are angry with me.

North Dakotans aren't known for their emotional displays; but I think I've learned enough to read the signs. They are subtle.

It's the sour look on someone's face as they pass me on the street. It's the person who avoids eye contact when talking to me. It's another person coming up to me in the grocery store and saying "John, I am angry with you."

Yes, subtle signs like these make me think you might be angry with me.

I have a few things to say to that. The first is "thank you."

I've been in North Dakota for thirteen months. (Fourteen of those were winter.) A little over a year but not really very much time in the grand scheme of things.

But in that short amount of time, you have welcomed me—in newspaper column form—into your homes over the last year and have let me try to entertain you. You let me poke fun at myself; poke fun at you; poke fun at the uniqueness that is rural North Dakota. Hopefully, you've laughed a time or two.

Many of you have also welcomed me—in me form—into your lives. You've let me into your activities; into your organizations; into your gossip. My time in North Dakota has meant a lot to me.

So thank you for being angry, upset or disappointed in me and my decision. It gives me the sense that I've meant something to you too.

Now that I have said "thank you" for being angry; I would also like to say, "please stop."

I know that when most people look at me they think: "Wow, what a macho superman." But the truth is I have a very thin skin.

When I hear "how can you leave?" in an angry tone, I want to believe that it's just that person's way of saying "we are really going to miss you." Instead, it feels like he is accusing me of kicking his dog. "Why? Why you heartless monster?"

So please stop being angry. My thin skin bruises very easily.

Please frame all future exchanges with me in the form of sadness, condolence, or krumkake. (I've still never had it, by the way.)

Since I'm already being so bold as to tell you what you can or cannot say to me, I would like to ask that you refrain from using the phrase, "just couldn't handle the winters, huh?"

For the record, I am not leaving North Dakota because of the harsh winters. I made it very clear in my last column that my departure is about my desire to work in the television industry; not my desire to get away from cold weather.

Yes, winter here is long and unbearable. But in this last year, I think I have proven that I can bear it. I may have been miserable part of that time and complaining all of that time; the truth remains that I can handle it.

Now that I've read you the riot act, you may be afraid to even broach the subject of my moving to California. That's OK too. I can talk about other stuff. I'm well-versed in many subjects. Just don't bring up politics. Or religion. Or sports. Or relationships.

Everything else is fair game. Here's how I imagine our conversation going:

ME: Hello.

NOT ME: Hello. Some weather we're having.

ME: O yah. I didn't expect it to be this hot the end of August.

NOT ME: Course when winter hits, we'll wish. . . oh never mind then.

ME: What's that you got there?

NOT ME: A plate of sandbakkels. Would you like one?

Joking aside, I am going to miss this place terribly. I'll write more about that in my next—and last—column. I sincerely hope and pray that this isn't a "good-bye" as much as it is a "see you in a bit."

I don't want to lose touch with the friends, near-friends and even fans that I have made in this last year. I plan to come back to visit. As soon as next year, I hope.

Just not until the winter's over. I couldn't bear another one of those.

photo: Gary M. Joraanstad

One more leaning abandoned building for your enjoyment.

HERE'S TO THE END OF AN ERROR, UM I MEAN 'ERA'

O! Pioneer column originally published 9/11/13

At this moment, as I write these words, there is a seed packet on top of my desk. The seed packet has been there for at least four months now. Radishes.

Awhile back, I decided that if I were going to write about life in North Dakota than I should write about ALL of life in North Dakota. And a good deal of life here is centered around farming. So I was going to become a farmer. I would need to start small since I don't own a farm. I don't even have a yard where I could plant a garden.

I was going to begin with a clay pot with some radish seeds. (I believe that's how Old MacDonald started out. E-i-e-i-o.)

This enterprise never got off the ground.

Several weekends ago, though, I had the opportunity to ride along in two different combines as they were harvesting—one was gathering spring wheat, the other canola. It was such a fun experience. And it's likely that this is the closest I'll ever come to being a farmer.

[I want to take a moment to thank Landy B., Alley K., and Ron J. for letting me ride along. And thank you to John F. for setting up the whole thing.]

In about a week, I will be heading out of North Dakota and moving back to Los Angeles—a place where the people don't even know what tater tot hot dish is. Uff-da.

I should probably take this last column to write about all of the things I will miss about this great state and the great little city that I've had the honor of living in for the last fourteen months. But it's too large a task. I couldn't possibly discuss all the people, places and experiences that have affected me in such a small amount of space. I would need the whole newspaper for that job. Scratch that: I would need a whole book.

Instead I'm going to mention some of the things I missed out on. Like my never-to-be farming career (or my dream of becoming a champion curler), a good many things that I will miss about North Dakota I never actually got in the first place.

I thought there would be a lot more pomp and fanfare when I arrived. I had this perception of a small town where everyone knew everyone; so whenever someone new moved in, he was lifted onto the townsfolk's shoulders and paraded down the town to cheers and applause.

I was wrong.

I moved to a place where strangers are looked at more with suspicion than celebration. Part of the reason for that is we are in the Bakken, where new people arrive every day. It's too much for locals to keep up with. The other part of it is: this area is filled with Norwegians. Norwegians live by the old motto "keep your friends at arms length and keep your strangers at an arm and a half."

I also thought moving to a small town would mean every eligible single lady in the county would be beating a path to my door. That didn't happen either. Unless they were beating that path in winter and just froze to death before they arrived at my door.

There are other things that I never experienced, not because they weren't available; but because I never took advantage of them. I never tried curling, or ice fishing, or hunting. I never got further north than Estevan or further south than Medora. I never played a round of golf at the country club or went to Burger night at the Moose Lodge in Crosby.

I have no one but myself to blame for that. There is a saying in my family (which I made up): "The Bayers are not doers." I had a lot of rich experiences while I lived in North Dakota; but all in all, I wish I had been more of a "doer." (And there is so much more to do here than I think even many locals realize.)

There are other experiences I missed. I never ate lutefisk, or assisted in the delivery of a calf, or attended a potluck dinner that included vegetables floating in Jell-o. So, not all missed experiences are a tragedy.

Well, I guess that wraps it up for me. It has been a joy and privilege writing this column, living in God's country and being a part of this community—even for this short time. To everyone who has touched my life, thank you for making my decision to leave such a difficult one. But now it is time for us to say good-bye to *O! Pioneer. . .*

Unless you want to buy my book: *O! Pioneer: My Year in North Dakota.* Coming to a bookstore near-ish you in time for Christmas. Assuming I get around to writing it.

photos: Jonell Bayer

In addition to putting out a newspaper, The Journal also serves as Crosby's office supply store/copy center. We use the Heidelberg press above to print numbers onto invoices and other business forms. The guillotine-looking thing I am standing by is our paper cutter.

We are very high tech.

CONCLUSION
SO WHAT'S THE POINT OF ALL THIS?

We will not cease from exploration,
and the end of all our exploring
will be to arrive where we started.
And know the place for the first time.
                    - T. S. Eliot

The words above are some of the most memorable lines from T. S. Eliot's poem, *The Wasteland*. They're beautiful and poignant and I have no idea what they mean. I'm a humor writer not a poem analyzer. But I've included these words because I think a book like this should end with something meaningful. And you certainly aren't going to get that from me. I'm a humor writer not a philosopher.

I like Eliot's bit about exploration. That's a major reason I moved to North Dakota. To explore—to go to a place I've never been, see what it's like to live in a small town, experience weather and people and weather and landscape and weather that I've never experienced before. My exploration certainly gave me many things. And it was a lot of fun, too.

The great joy of writing *O! Pioneer* was hearing how much people enjoyed reading it. Every week, someone new would stop me on the street or come into the newspaper to say nice things about my stupid little column. One thing I heard a lot was: "You've only lived here a few months and already you *get* us."

For me, that is the highest praise I could have received. I just don't know how true it is.

Take the previous essay, for example. The last column I wrote for the newspaper. It wasn't until after it went to press, that I realized that I'd committed a major faux pas.

You don't see it now because I went back and fixed it. But in the column as it originally ran, I committed the third greatest sin that you can commit in North Dakota. I thanked people! Publicly! By name! First *and* last name!

In all likelihood, after that column ran, those men could no longer show their faces in town because of the embarrassment. They would know that people are thinking that they're the kind of men who do things to draw attention to themselves. And I can only imagine the shame that I've brought on their families.

(For those who might be wondering: the two sins bigger than that one are murder and hugging where people can see you.)

That business above about publicly thanking someone is sort of a joke —sort of—but it still illustrates a bittersweet truth. While I lived in North Dakota, I always liked and enjoyed the people, but most of the time I didn't feel like *one* of the people.

North Dakotans have a reputation—one that I've worked tirelessly to promote—for being unemotional, distant, aloof. And that probably has something to do with my own feeling of disconnection.

But the truth is, I was as unemotional, distant and aloof as anyone else I might have met. From day one, I was in this for the short haul, so I didn't make the effort to go from being in the community to being part of the community—to move past friendly to friend.

I like to accuse North Dakotans of holding people at arm's length. But when I look down, it's my arm that's in the air.

For the record—I admire the hell out of the people of North Dakota.

They have a strength of character and of will that I hope has rubbed off on me at least a little bit. This strength was evident right from the beginning.

My plane landed in Minot on July 17, 2012. I was picked up from the airport by Holly and her brother Stan. Before taking me to my new home of Crosby, Stan drove us around Minot to get a look at the devastation.

The previous summer, there had been major flooding in this part of North Dakota. The home I lived at in Crosby had been flooded out. The carpeting was new and almost all of the furniture was up on wood blocks in fear of "the next time."

But Minot got the worst of it. The rain on its own was enough to flood many homes, but when the Souris River filled to capacity and beyond, it ravaged the place. Over 11,000 acres and 4,000 homes were flooded. Some 11,000 people were evacuated in a city of 40,000 people.

A year later, as I saw North Dakota for the first time, I learned everything I needed to know about this place and its people.

They are proud. As we drove through Minot, we saw hundreds of houses that were still unoccupied—either the damage hadn't been fixed yet, or the residents simply hadn't returned yet. But in each yard was the same yellow sign: *I'm Coming Back!*

Usually, when there's a natural disaster in this country, the news is all over it. But I didn't recall this story getting any national attention at the time. (In researching this book, I found a few news stories online. Not much. One major network reported that there had been flooding in Minot, *South* Dakota.) A flood of water is often followed by a flood of attention, then a flood of money and relief workers from around the country. I'm sure there was some, but I'm also sure there wasn't enough.

And on some level, that's just fine with North Dakota. "I'd rather do it myself" is the state motto. Help is something you give—it's not something you get. They'll take the help if it's offered, but they don't want to put anyone out.

We saw FEMA trailers scattered about, and I thought how tough it must be to live in one of those for over a year. Then Stan realized that one grouping of FEMA trailers was actually a man camp put there by some oil company. So the next 20 minutes was occupied with the game—*Displaced*

Homeowner or Oil Field Worker?

They are determined. I'd rather say, "They are fighters" but that implies that North Dakotans are looking for a fight. They are not. But when faced with adversity, North Dakotans will do whatever it takes to get it done.

Those yellow signs that read "*I'm Coming Back!*" were designed so that the middle word could be torn off and the sign would stay intact. So for every three or four signs that read "*I'm Coming Back!*" you'd see a sign in front of one home that let us know "*I'm Back!*" A lot of people had to leave their homes, but I bet almost all of them are back now. It took awhile but once a North Dakotan is set on something. . .

They know a good thing when they've got it. Here's my guess: the reason all of those people who had to leave came back is because they knew there's no place better than North Dakota. And they're right. Of all the places I've lived, North Dakota has the strongest sense of family, the strongest sense of community, the strongest sense of its identity than anywhere else.

Life in North Dakota is simpler—not easier, just simpler. Every day I got up with the knowledge of what I needed to do that day and how to do it. I had a fairly good grasp of the places that I'd go and the people I'd see that day. At the end of the day I'd return home satisfied, having accomplished all that I needed to do.

At the risk of getting churchy, I'm going to refer to some words from the Apostle Paul. (My Catholic brethren call him St. Paul, but we informal Protestants prefer to think of Paul as just a really nice guy.) Paul wrote: "Make it your ambition to lead a quiet life, to mind your own business and to work with your hands, just as we told you, so that your daily life may win the respect of outsiders and so that you will not be dependent on anybody." That seems like a pretty nice deal, even if you're a religious person.

This guy Paul was writing to people in a place called Thessalonica, but he might as well have been working for the ND Tourism Board. He is describing life there. It's a quiet life. (Quiet, not easy.) People mind their own business. Most work with their hands. And the two most prized possessions are independence and respect. ("So if that sounds like the life for you, come on down . . .er, up. . . to North Dakota today!" This message brought to you by the NDTB.)

That's my "North Dakota in a nutshell." It turns out, I knew all of this on some level way back on that first day driving through Minot.

I guess T.S. Eliot knew what he was talking about with that arriving where we started and knowing that place for the first time.

"So if North Dakota's so great, why did you leave?"

That's a great question. I wish I had a great answer for it. I guess, to paraphrase Eliot, I'm just not yet "at the end of all my exploring."

Also, did I mention the endless winter?

photos: Holly R. Anderson,
John Bayer

A few final photos to remind you that North Dakota is mostly just frozenness. The above photos, as well as the two pictures on the cover, were taken on March 20, 2013.

The first day of Spring.

Made in the USA
San Bernardino, CA
15 September 2018